FRANKLIN D. ROOSEVELT
and the New Deal

BY SHARON SHEBAR

Illustrations by Gary Lippincott

Barron's Educational Series, Inc.
New York/London/Toronto/Sydney

First edition published in 1987
by Barron's Educational Series, Inc.

© Copyright 1987 by Eisen, Durwood & Co., Inc.
Cover art copyright © 1987 Burt Silverman
Cover design by Wendy Palitz.

All inquiries should be addressed to:
Barron's Educational Series, Inc.
250 Wireless Blvd.
Hauppauge, NY 11788

Library of Congress Catalog Card No. 87-21456

International Standard Book No. 0-8120-3916-5

Library of Congress Cataloging-in-Publication Data

Shebar, Sharon Sigmond.
  Franklin Delano Roosevelt and the New Deal / Sharon Shebar :
  illustrations by Gary Lippincott. — 1st ed.
  p. cm. — (Henry Steele Commager's Americans)
  Includes index.
  Summary: A biography of the thirty-second President, the only one
to be elected to a fourth term, who began the New Deal to counteract
the effects of the Depression.
  ISBN 0-8120-3916-5
  1. Roosevelt, Franklin D. (Franklin Delano), 1882-1945 — Juvenile
literature. 2. New Deal, 1933-1945 — Juvenile literature. 3. United
States — Politics and government — 1933-1945 — Juvenile literature.
4. Presidents — United States — Biography — Juvenile literature.
[1. Roosevelt, Franklin D. (Franklin Delano), 1882-1945.
2. Presidents. 3. New Deal, 1933-1945. 4. United States — Politics
and government — 1933-1945.] I. Shebar, Sharon. II. Lippincott,
Gary, ill. III. Title. IV. Series.
E807.S43 1987
973.917'092'4 — dc19   87-21456
[B]   CIP
[92]   AC

Printed in the United States of America

7 8 9 0   9 6 9 3   9 8 7 6 5 4 3 2 1

CONTENTS

CONTENTS

Franklin Delano Roosevelt came to the Presidency at a time when the nation faced the greatest crisis since the Civil War and responded to it as resolutely as Lincoln had responded to that earlier challenge. Early in Herbert Hoover's administration, the nation had been plunged into the longest and most desperate depression in our history—The Great Depression—which afflicted every segment of society. Bankers and industrialists suffered as well as farmers and working men and women. Where Hoover had done nothing but look hopefully for a turn in the economic tide, which never came, Roosevelt acted with confident courage and efficiency. On his first day in the White House he proclaimed a bank holiday to fend off disastrous "runs" on the nation's banks, and asked the Congress for authority to wage war on the depression as if it were a foreign foe.

His Inaugural Address called for a "New Deal," and that is what he persuaded the Congress and the American people to give him. Almost every day Congress was confronted with some new far-reaching proposal designed to reduce the effects of the depression, to provide relief for its stricken victims, and to make the government an efficient servant of the *whole* people, not just of isolated segments. What this came to was modest enough by Old World standards, but was considered revolutionary by many Americans. They had forgotten that the United

States Constitution twice mandates concern for the "general welfare" as well as for the "common defense." Roosevelt was determined to bring American policies on social welfare up to the standard which existed in most Old World countries. In this he largely succeeded. Insofar as we now have a "welfare state," the credit belongs to the first two Roosevelt administrations.

The second administration was shadowed by the crisis of totalitarianism in Germany, Italy, and Japan. In 1939, the crisis erupted into the largest and most destructive war in history. Forseeing the probability that the United States would be drawn into the conflict, Roosevelt turned his energies to arousing the nation to its peril. He encouraged rearmament and an active diplomatic effort to support Old World democracies. After Pearl Harbor, the United States officially entered the war and Winston Churchill could thank God that Britain would live, democracy would live. It was the tremendous material strength of the United States and the vision, the energy and the courage of Roosevelt that turned the tide and, in the end, brought down the totalitarian powers. Throughout the long conflict, Roosevelt worked to create a peaceful world after the war. He lived to see the collapse of Fascist Italy and Nazi Germany, and to know that Imperial Japan, too, was doomed to defeat. Sadly, he died before the creation of the United Nations, and the peaceful postwar world he wanted so much to see.

Henry Steele Commager
Amherst, Massachusetts

CHAPTER ONE

A Splendid Baby Boy

J ames Roosevelt sat stiffly in his chair and clenched his fists. The morning of January 30, 1882, was freezing cold. Bare trees shivered in the icy wind blowing off the Hudson River.

Sara Roosevelt, James's pregnant wife, lay in the mahogany bed before him. Servants moved quietly through the room, carrying out the orders of a worried-looking doctor. Sara had been in labor for 36 hours, much longer than normal. The mother and her unborn child were now in great danger from exhaustion and too much anesthetic.

Sara, one of the five beautiful Delano sisters, had married James two years before. He was a widower with a full-grown son named Rosy. She had been twenty-seven and he had been fifty-two. Sara's parents had been startled by her choice of a husband. How could such a lovely young girl marry such an old man? Sara, who was as strong willed as she was beautiful, had refused to listen. "He may not be the youngest man I know," she said of her husband, "but he is certainly the finest." Their marriage was a happy one. Now, James Roosevelt faced the horrible possibility of losing both Sara and their child.

1

A scream came from the bed—the wail of a newborn infant. James breathed a deep sigh of relief. He stood over the bed and, for the first time, looked into the face of his new son. Later he wrote in his wife's diary: "At quarter to nine my Sara had a splendid large baby boy. He weighs ten pounds without clothes." They named the baby Franklin, after his mother's uncle.

The house baby Franklin was born into was pleasant and luxurious. The Roosevelts, like most Hudson Valley families, were quite rich. James had been president of a railroad company. Now, at fifty-four, he had left his job and he spent his days taking care of Springwood, the family estate. With his mutton-chop sideburns, twinkling eyes, and old-fashioned good manners, James Roosevelt was the picture of a country gentleman.

Sara Delano Roosevelt was every inch a lady. Tall and graceful, she was known for her perfect manners. One friend wrote that she "acted like a queen." Even as a very young girl, she had been serious and strong-minded. She had been well-bred, and she was determined to raise her son in the same manner.

When the January frost gave way to spring, Sara Roosevelt was well enough to take on the care of her baby. She refused to hand him over to a nurse or nanny, as was the custom of the day. Perhaps because Franklin's birth had been so difficult, she was unwilling to let anyone else take care of him.

Franklin was a healthy, pretty baby. He was plump and rosy, with long golden curls. His father wrote of him that "He is . . . always happy. Not crying, worrying."

2

F.D.R. on father's shoulders

Sara dressed him in long lace dresses (the current fashion). He grew quickly and, to his mother's delight, proved to be a very good-tempered and clever child. As soon as he was old enough to explore on his own, he was taken by his father around the grounds of Springwood.

Springwood was a fairy-tale setting. The sprawling old mansion was set in a thousand acres of rolling green countryside. Hand in hand with his father, Franklin toured the rose garden, the vegetable patch, and the pigs, lambs, and goats in the animal pens. Franklin loved the dark stables where the glossy-skinned race horses stood quietly in their neat stalls. His father told them of races they had won, and how fast they could gallop. James explained to Franklin how every part of Springwood worked: when the vegetables were planted; how to prune the apple trees, or feed a baby lamb. He wanted his son to learn how a farm was run.

Franklin listened solemnly. He was a shy child who clung closely to his parents. His mother, especially, was the most important presence in his life. Springwood was large and mysterious without her. He was afraid to go into the large and bustling kitchen without her. Instead he would stand at the threshold, timidly peeking through the door. Even the friendliest maids could not get him to say so much as a word unless his mother was beside him.

She usually was. As Franklin grew older, his mother's fierce attachment to him deepened. He was her "angel," her "treasure," and both she and James showered their son with attention and affection. It was small wonder that, for Franklin (as he later wrote), "Hyde Park was the center of the world."

Yet the Roosevelts did not spend all their time there. Like many wealthy people of the time, they often went on long trips. Each year they sailed for Germany where James, who had a bad heart, would "take the cure" at Nauheim, one of the famous mineral springs of Europe. In those days, such mineral springs or "waters" were thought to cure all kinds of illness, from headaches to

Campobello—summer home

lameness. Nauheim was full of invalids, but nevertheless a most elegant resort. Franklin was wide-eyed at the ladies and gentlemen he saw there—all dressed in clothes of lace and fine silks and satins such as he had never seen in Springwood. Each afternoon, he and his parents drank tea on the terrace of the hotel, while a band played waltzes and German folk songs.

Summers were something else altogether. The family set out for their summer home on the small island of Campobello, off the coast of Canada. The house at Campobello was large and simple, the island breezy and pine scented, with beautiful spots for picnics and walks. It was small enough that Franklin soon knew every corner of it, including where you could pick wild blueberries and

5

strawberries. Best of all, Campobello's features, as far as he was concerned, was the sea—the bright, blue Atlantic Ocean, which stretched as far as the eye could see in every direction.

It was at Campobello that Franklin learned to love the sea. Soon it was "in his blood." Franklin was always surrounded by the sights and sounds of ships. The Delanos had all been sea-faring men and their old house, Algonac, was right beside the docks. Its rooms were filled with sea-faring souvenirs—brass cannons, sailor hats, and model ships. No wonder Franklin dreamed of sailing the sea. It was at Campobello that he was taken out on a real ship for the very first time. It was aboard his father's yacht, the *New Moon*. James held Franklin's hand as the ship sailed out of the bay. Then he showed his small son around the wooden deck and showed him how a sailboat worked, hoisting the sails until the boat fairly skimmed over the calm water.

From the first, Franklin was thrilled by sailing. The mysterious tangles of ropes fascinated him. He listened to the orders his father shouted back and forth to the crew. He sniffed at the salt taste of the air, and put his face to the wind. "I'm going to be a sailor when I grow up," he announced to his father.

Franklin now spoke endlessly of ships and brave men who traveled the seas of the world. He made his mother cut off his long curls and dress him in a sailor suit. When the family returned to Hyde Park, Franklin's favorite game was pretending to command a ship from his "crow's nest"—a tree house his father had made for him in an old hemlock tree in the garden.

While his dreams were of sailing, Franklin Roosevelt's daily life followed a steady routine. Little changed and little varied. Meals were served by quiet, polite servants, who cleared away the dishes, as soon as the meal was done. The gardens were beautifully kept, and the living room furniture gleamed with polish. It was a life of luxury. Franklin did not yet realize that not everyone lived this way. He knew nothing of poverty and misfortune.

In later life, he remembered his childhood as the most peaceful and secure time of his life. "Thinking back to my earliest days," he wrote when he was much older, "I am impressed by the peacefulness and regularity of things . . . "

It was the peace of the rich and powerful. The Roosevelts knew everybody who was anybody, and everywhere they went they were welcomed. One day when Franklin was five years old, he was made to take off his sailor suit and dress in his best clothes. It was a special occasion. The Roosevelts were going to Washington, D.C. to visit Grover Cleveland, president of the United States.

While Grover Cleveland and his father discussed politics, Franklin sat quietly in the corner of the president's office, snacking on milk and cake. Franklin later remembered the president as the largest man he had ever seen. When it was time to go, the shy little boy was brought forward to shake the president's hand. Looking down at the child, the president said an odd thing.

"My little man," he told Franklin, "I am making a strange wish for you. It is that you may never be president of the United States."

"What did Mr. President mean?" Franklin asked his father as they were leaving. Simply that "being president of the United States is a very difficult job indeed!" his father replied, looking down with a smile. Franklin listened and nodded. It probably seemed to him then, as it did to everyone around him, that he would grow up to be what his father was: a "country gentleman." His mother, Sara, certainly wanted nothing else for him. "The life of a gentleman," she said, "is the highest ideal I could hold up before our boy."

Franklin Roosevelt did grow up to be a "country gentleman," and a city gentleman too. Yet, in a way neither he nor anyone around him could imagine, he was to be seen as a traitor to Hyde Park and all that it stood for. The world he was to help shape was to be very different from the quiet mansions and sprawling green lawns of his childhood. It was to be a world that would include a great depression, bread lines, unemployment, slums, and war.

CHAPTER TWO

The Good, Obedient Child

On the surface it did not seem likely that Franklin Delano Roosevelt would grow up to change the world. His early life was orderly and traditional. Like most children of the rich, Franklin was educated at home. However, unlike many children of his class who were allowed to run free until they went away to boarding school, Franklin's time at home was rigidly organized. His mother made herself responsible for his education. Her standards were high. When he was six, she set him the following schedule:

7:00 A.M.—Get up, Get Dressed
8:00 A.M.—Breakfast
9:00–12:00 A.M.—Morning lessons
12:00–1:00 P.M.—Play outside
1:00–2:00 P.M.—Lunch
2:00–4:00 P.M.—Afternoon Lessons

He was to follow it until he was fourteen. Soon a series of governesses were brought in to teach Franklin his lessons.

His favorite teacher was a Frenchwoman called Mademoiselle Sandoz. She was a tiny thing—not much big-

9

Boyhood activities

ger than Franklin himself—but lively and enthusiastic. Pupil and teacher soon became fast friends. She interested him in history and French, and he convinced her to race up and down the long winding corridors of Springwood.

"How Franklin could run up and down that corridor," she later wrote, "making me run with him until I was breathless."

Mme. Sandoz returned to France to marry, and Franklin's other governesses were not nearly as close friends with their young pupil as she had been. Usually a "model child," Franklin was often hard on his governesses. He played practical jokes on each of them, and later liked to say he had "driven one governess to the madhouse, and another to matrimony."

But during those years—and ever after—the strongest influence on him remained his mother.

It was Sara who listened to him and encouraged him. It was she who first got him interested in stamp collecting, bird watching and natural history.

Franklin was a born collector. He could not bear to throw anything away, and soon his desk was piled high with stamps. He would pore over the brightly colored stamps with their strange pictures of kings, queens and faraway places for hours. He dreamed of visiting all the countries in his stamp collection. He picked out the countries on his stamps from a map of the world pinned up over his bed. To his mother's delight, Franklin learned a great deal of geography this way (not to mention a little history).

Stamp collecting was a hobby Sara wholeheartedly

approved of. But there was another hobby Franklin took up that Sara did not like at all, and that was hunting. Franklin's father loved to hunt, and by the time Franklin was ten he was begging for a shotgun. His mother was appalled. Guns were awful things! Franklin would kill himself! Franklin persisted. Writing indirectly to his mother in an essay called *Guns and Squirrels* he argued his case:

> "Many mamas think guns are very dangerous things and think they will go off without cartridges or without being cocked, but if properly handled they are not . . . "

His mother gave in. For his eleventh birthday, Franklin was given a gun of his very own.

He began to haunt the woods around Springwood. He even began a diary recording all his triumphs. "Shot a Pine Finch today!" he wrote proudly, or, "This afternoon I bagged a Barred Owl with a single shot!" Sara did not like his enthusiasm one bit. He seemed to prefer hunting to anything else! It was the only sign of rebelliousness in the "model child."

But even the hunting served a useful purpose. Franklin became interested in taxidermy—stuffing and mounting specimens of the birds and animals he shot. Like his distant cousin, Theodore Roosevelt, he decided to start a "natural history museum"—a collection of stuffed birds and animals, all his own. But skinning and mounting birds for his collection was not as much fun as he'd thought it would be. Many of the chemicals made him

12

feel sick! He stuck it out as long as he could, but before long he was sending his specimens to a professional taxidermist. Despite this setback, the "Franklin Roosevelt Natural History Museum" grew and grew. His mother did not approve, but she could not help but be proud of his skill. By the age of fourteen, Franklin had collected and identified over three hundred different birds of the region. His grandfather, Warren Delano, had him made a lifetime member of the New York Museum of Natural History!

Franklin impressed everyone who met him as a serious and well-behaved boy. This was not surprising. He had spent his entire life surrounded by adults who gave him nothing but attention and encouragement. He knew little of boys his own age and almost nothing of the world outside Springwood, and the Roosevelt summer island, Campobello. All that was soon to change. For, as his fourteenth birthday approached, his father decided it was time for Franklin to go away to school.

The school had been chosen years before. It was one of the most famous schools in the country—Groton Academy in Connecticut. Franklin should have gone there at twelve, but his mother Sara had begged her husband not to send Franklin away. Now, even she felt they had no choice. To be a proper gentleman, Franklin would have to go to school. On a cool, crisp September morning in 1896, Sara, dressed all in black, led her son to the horse-drawn carriage that would carry them down the long winding driveway to the train station, and from there, away to a new world.

CHAPTER THREE

A Proper Education

A t that time Groton was the creation of one man, its headmaster, the Reverend Endicott Peabody. He was a tall man with piercing eyes and a strong, deep voice that commanded instant respect. To the boys at Groton, he was a father figure. They longed for his approval, but were a little afraid of him as well. Although the sons of the richest men in America went to Groton, the Reverend Peabody did not believe in spoiling his pupils. He believed in building character.

Groton was modeled on an English public school. The boys were kept busy. No moment of their day was unscheduled, for the Reverend Peabody believed that "the curse of American school life is loafing." The day began at 6:45 A.M. and ended with a firm "lights out" after evening chapel. In between, there was scarcely a free moment from classes, study halls, sports, and school assemblies. Even the decoration of the dormitories reflected the stern discipline of the place. The boys slept in tiny six-by-nine-foot cubicles. They were not allowed to hang pictures in their rooms. There were no closets. There were no doors, but only curtains, because the headmaster

Groton—F.D.R.'s prep school

felt too much privacy was bad for "the moral character." For Franklin, who was used to Sara's rules and regulations, life at Groton was not a complete shock. But other boys found it hard to get used to their new home. Headmaster Peabody often told the story of a New York millionaire's son who was found crying the first day at Groton. When asked what was wrong, he replied, "But Sir, there are no carpets on the stairs!" Headmaster Peabody was determined to make such rich young boys into good Christians who had the proper moral quality to lead the nation.

Because Franklin had entered the school at fourteen, he was two years behind the other boys his age. He was assigned to the dormitory for twelve year olds.

He was not a success. He found the younger boys childish, and they said he was a "wet blanket!" Franklin spoke with a slightly English accent. The other Grotonians (who had an accent all their own) found his way of speaking ridiculous. "It's Master Franklin," they would crow whenever he walked by. Franklin was shocked. He'd always gotten along with everyone. What was wrong? He did his best to be a good student. As each class opened, there was Franklin right in the front row, his pen poised over his paper. But this sort of behavior only made the other boys dislike him even more. "That Roosevelt is a brown-noser!" they whispered to one another. "Sissy!" Franklin could not understand it. It got so bad that when he finally did get in trouble for talking in class, he wrote to his mother: "I am very glad of it, as I was thought to have no school spirit before!"

Adolescent boys, unlike the adults he had known, could be cruel for no particular reason. One day, a group of older boys pounced on Franklin, jabbing him with their hockey sticks. They forced him to dance for them. Blushing bright red, Franklin did as they asked. But it was an incident the sensitive, "well-behaved" boy was never to forget.

Athletic skill was important to social success at Groton. The most popular boys at Groton were the football
players. "They were treated like heroes," wrote one former pupil. Franklin longed to be a success, and he tried
out for all the teams. But he was just not a born athlete.
He was too thin for the football team. He could not pitch
or catch well enough for the baseball team. As for crew,
he was too big to be a good coxswain and too small to
be an oarsman. After weeks of tryouts, he finally got a
place on the fourth-place scrub football team. It was not
much of an honor. They were the worst team in the
school. Their only games were against the third-place
scrub football team, who, while not much better, usually
managed to beat them.

It was a discouraging start. Franklin began to wonder
if he would ever fit in, and what (if anything) he was
good at.

Unfortunately, the only thing he proved really good
at his first term at Groton was getting sick. Because he
had never spent much time with other children, he had
not built up immunities to normal childhood diseases. If
any boy at Groton came down with anything, Franklin
was sure to get it. He had colds and sore throats, fevers
and flus. He spent much of that fall lying miserably in
quarantine in the dusty brown infirmary which everyone
at Groton called "The Pest House."

He had a new nickname too, "Uncle Frank," and it
was not flattering. Franklin was given the nickname because Taddy, the eldest son of his half-brother Rosy, was
also at Groton. Although Taddy was several years older

than Franklin, he was officially Franklin's nephew. This amused the other boys, especially since, as they said, "Franklin acts like an old man anyway." Worse still, Taddy was not popular with anyone, and was mercilessly teased by even the youngest boys at Groton. Franklin thought that by calling him "Uncle Frank" the other boys were saying he was as bad as Taddy.

So Franklin's first term at Groton was far from pleasant. From his tiny dormitory cubicle, or his room in the infirmary, Franklin counted the months and weeks. When the end of term came, he was only too happy to escape to New York City to join his mother and father for the midterm holiday.

Even the holiday in New York was not the restful vacation he had hoped it would be. Franklin's father looked much older. James Roosevelt's heart was growing worse. He could no longer get around by himself. He coughed endlessly, and his face was pale and drawn. His mother did not discuss James's health with Franklin, but she was clearly worried. Franklin felt as if the rug was being pulled out from under his feet. He was more reserved and quieter when he returned to Groton. His eyes now had a serious look. He felt he was growing up, and the world he was growing into confused and troubled him.

At least Groton improved a little the second term. Franklin joined the debating team and the campus newspaper, the *Grotonian*. Here, at last, he made a place for himself. His mature style of speaking and writing, which had once made the other boys laugh at him, now proved an asset. He began to win debates. Soon his articles dotted the pages of the paper. Even his athletic life began to look up. He became a proud member of the BBBB, the Bum Base Ball Boys. "We are about the worst players in the school!" he proudly wrote his mother. They won some hard-fought victories that season against their main rivals, the Carter's Little Liver Pills.

Franklin now had a best friend, a boy much like him named Lothrop Brown. Together, Lothrop and Franklin managed to get into all sorts of trouble and they shared a common hero—Franklin's cousin, Theodore Roosevelt.

At that time, Theodore Roosevelt was just becoming a major figure in American politics. He was a hearty, robust man with lots of energy and a desire to reform everything under the sun. Teddy Roosevelt spoke out against the terrible conditions in the slums of New York and Chicago. He criticized the corruption of big city government. He argued passionately for the rights of the "common working man." This was a new direction in American politics and Teddy Roosevelt was at the center of it. His activities scandalized Franklin's mother, Sara. She felt that a gentleman and a Roosevelt should have better things to do with his time than mess about with politics. Franklin could not help admiring his energetic cousin. And now Teddy was involved in a new escapade, something that all the boys at Groton found exciting: war.

In 1898, newspapers all across America were full of news of Cuba's fight with Spain. For over three years, the tiny island had been fighting to be free of Spanish rule. They had asked the United States for help, but President McKinley wanted to stay out of it. Then something happened to change that. An American battleship, the *Maine*, was blown up in Havana harbor. Two hundred American sailors were killed. Rumors swept the country that the Spanish had done it. It was time to fight.

The slogan "Remember the Maine!" swept the nation. Men lined up to volunteer for combat. .The ranks of the military swelled. The Spanish-American War began.

Theodore Roosevelt was right in the center of it. Not the type to sit at home, he had put together his own command, "The Rough Riders." He led them in a victorious charge up San Juan Hill in Cuba. The Rough Riders worshiped their commander, and nicknamed him "T.R." Soon Teddy Roosevelt's bespectacled and moustached face was staring out of posters all across the country. Franklin and thousands of other young boys longed to be just like him.

Later, Franklin told a story about this period. Unlike other boys, who merely dreamed of joining the fight, Franklin and Lothrop came up with a concrete plan: they would run away from Groton, hop a train to Boston, and enlist! First they needed a way to escape. They remembered that, twice a week, a local baker came to Groton to sell his fresh-baked pies. Franklin had an inspiration. "All we have to do," he whispered to Lothrop in study hall, "is pay the man to smuggle us away in his van!" Lothrop hesitated. They were only sixteen. What if the Navy refused to take them? Franklin, who considered himself an expert sailor, convinced Lothrop that they had nothing to fear. "Listen here," he boasted, "I know more than enough sea-lore to be an officer. In any case, it's our duty!" Lothrop agreed. The pieman was contacted and everything was set.

But the night before the pieman was to come, both boys began to feel weak and feverish. "We're just nervous!" Franklin insisted as he grew dizzier and dizzier. Soon little red spots began to appear all over their bodies. It was scarlet fever! One of the teachers noticed. Against their will, both boys were ordered into the Pest House. They were to be in quarantine for six weeks.

In those days, scarlet fever was a dangerous disease, and many people died of it. The school sent a telegram to Franklin's parents, who were away in Europe. Sara rushed back to be with her son. But when she arrived at Pest House she was forbidden to enter, for scarlet fever was highly contagious. Not even family members could see the patients. Sara was indignant. "I am a Roosevelt," she informed the doctor. No one was going to stop her from seeing her son. She marched out of the infirmary and searched the school grounds until she found an old ladder. This she placed against the window of Franklin's sickroom and was soon perched right on top of it, speaking animatedly with her son through the open window.

Franklin healed slowly. He kept up with the war through newspapers, and magazines and prayed that he would get better before it was all over. His prayers were not answered. Spain surrendered two months later and before he knew it, Franklin was back in the Groton routine.

His remaining years at Groton passed without incident. The most dramatic thing that happened was that he had to get glasses. Determined to be like "T.R." in one way or another, Franklin insisted on a pair of gold-rimmed pince-nez spectacles, exactly like those his cousin wore. He wore them for the rest of his life.

While his last years at Groton were peaceful, Franklin never entirely got over his initial unhappiness there. In later life he was to praise Headmaster Peabody and carry with him forever Peabody's ideas of what a good Christian man should be. Yet he was also to remember, bitterly, how the other boys had rejected him. At Groton, Franklin said, "Something had gone sadly wrong." He had expected to fit in. He had expected to be a success, and he had failed. Perhaps he was not the perfect gentleman his mother wanted him to be. In June of 1900, however, Franklin Delano Roosevelt was not too worried about this. He had other things to think about. He was leaving Groton's stately courtyards forever. He was going to Harvard!

CHAPTER FOUR

Harvard Days

F ranklin entered Harvard eagerly. Harvard, the nation's oldest and most prestigious university, stood in the center of Cambridge, Massachusetts, just across the river from the bustling excitement of Boston. The handsome, ivy-colored buildings promised a wealth of new experiences. Franklin was determined to make the most of them. Full of enthusiasm, he resolved to put the loneliness and humiliation he had suffered at Groton firmly behind him.

He was rooming with his old friend, Lothrop Brown, in the elegant "gold coast" dormitories. The two had real gentlemen's quarters—a suite of sunny, wood-paneled rooms which they decorated with beer steins and Groton pennants. Franklin bought a suit of evening clothes, several new pairs of shoes, and, as a final touch, a brand new straw derby. He was ready to enter the social whirl. And what a whirl it was! There were festivities at clubs on campus, and dances, and parties on Beacon Hill, the neighborhood of Boston's wealthiest citizens. Here, Franklin met the society girls of the day, and quickly developed a reputation of being a playboy.

But Franklin was determined to do more than be popular at parties. He wanted to make a name for himself on campus. One way of doing this was getting involved in Harvard's legendary campus newspaper, the *Crimson*.

Working on the *Grotonian* had given Franklin a taste for newspaper work. At Groton he had been happiest digging up a story. He desperately wanted to get on the staff of the *Crimson*, but competition for a freshman reporter's job was stiff. There were five places available for freshman editors and sixty-two boys in the running. Franklin would have to do something to prove he was the best choice. But what? He needed a good story.

Then he had a lucky break.

He learned that his cousin, Theodore Roosevelt, now vice-president of the United States, was staying overnight at Professor Lawrence Lowell's house. He called up to say "Hello." During their conversation, he learned that T.R. was lecturing at Lowell's class on government at nine o'clock the next morning. The lecture was being kept a secret, to keep away the crowds. As Franklin hung up the phone, it occurred to him that *this* was his story!

His heart beating, the would-be reporter raced across Harvard Yard to the *Crimson* offices. The story appeared early the next morning, and soon the entire school knew that the notorious Theodore Roosevelt would actually be lecturing on campus.

By nine o'clock the next morning, an enormous crowd had gathered in front of Sanders Theatre, where Lowell's class was to meet. Lowell was furious. Teddy Roosevelt found it amusing.

It was hardly the scoop of the century, and Franklin was well aware that he had gotten the story through family connections. Nevertheless, it was enough. He was now a strong candidate to be chosen for the *Crimson.* There was no happier, more excited boy at Harvard.

Although Franklin kept himself busy his first term trying to be a success at Harvard, this success did not have much to do with education. Between his social life and his newspaper work there was little time for studying. Franklin's average his first term was only a C+. He was to make the same grades throughout his entire career at Harvard. He was not very interested in his classes. As he told a friend, they were "like an electric light without any wire. You need a lamp for light, but it's useless if you can't switch it on." He was already more interested in "real work," particularly the newspaper. As the term wore on, he found himself spending more and more time in the *Crimson's* shabby, comfortable offices.

Near the end of his first term, something happened to disrupt his newfound happiness. In November his father, James, suffered another heart attack. This time it was even more serious. When Franklin was told of it, he wanted to go see his father immediately. His mother told him to wait. He was not sent for until December 4, and by then it was clear that James Roosevelt did not have much longer to live. Three days later, James Roosevelt died in the company of his wife and son.

That Christmas was a sad one. When Franklin returned to Harvard for spring term, he felt that he had become an adult. He was now responsible for his heartbroken mother. The term passed slowly and the summer was long and difficult. In September, something unex-

F.D.R.'s mother, Sara

pected happened: President McKinley was assassinated,
and Theodore Roosevelt was now president of the United
States. Franklin began now, more than ever, to identify
with Theodore, and with politics. He began to think of
a political career.

This newfound seriousness did not last long. Franklin was a Harvard sophomore now, and the all-important

ritual of being chosen for a club lay before him. Franklin was eager to meet the challenge.

In those days, all young gentlemen belonged to a social club. The clubs ate together, studied together, and gave parties together. Each club had a house of its own which served as a social center for its members. Joining a club was crucial to one's social success. The most exclusive club of all, the one Franklin desperately wanted to join, was the Porcellian. His father had belonged to it, as had his cousin Theodore. To Franklin, the Porcellian represented true success—the success he had failed to achieve at Groton. It was a prize he was determined to win. In January, Franklin began the long process that was required for a young gentleman to gain admittance to the Porcellian's hallowed doors.

His roommate, Lothrop Brown was chosen as a member. It seemed only a matter of days before Franklin, too, would be chosen. Then Franklin was told that he had been blackballed.

Blackballing was the way new applicants were rejected. The members of the club had held a meeting. Each member was given two balls, one black and one white. They placed one of the balls, black or white, into a ballot box. One black ball was all it took to make a candidate unacceptable to the club.

Franklin later described his rejection from the Porcellian as "the greatest disappointment of my life." He never found out why he had been rejected. It bewildered him as it had at Groton, only this time, he never recovered from it. It meant he would never live up to his family's idea of him. He would never be the perfect aristocrat. Later, certain wealthy men would say the "New Deal" policies Franklin put into effect when he became president were a way of revenging himself on the Porcellain.

The setback was made worse by the fact that his mother, Sara, had recently moved to Boston to be close to her son. Now that her husband was gone, she wanted to share in her son's busy life. It was humiliating for Franklin to have to tell her about his rejection from the Porcellian, especially as his mother could not understand it. Roosevelts were winners. They rejected other people. Other people did not reject them.

To get over the Porcellian episode, Franklin threw himself with renewed ardor into his newspaper work. He now spent most of his time in the offices of the *Crimson*. He decided to become a real newspaperman. Through his reporting, he became exposed to a Harvard beyond that of the gentlemen's clubs and the social circuit. He began to see that not all boys at Harvard were rich. The poorer students had to work to pay for their schooling. Unlike Franklin and Lothrop, they did not live in luxurious suites, but in cramped, unsafe dorm rooms on Harvard Yard. These poorer boys did not get to join the clubs, or even run for political office in the university. Franklin became concerned about these issues, and wrote about them in the *Crimson*.

Franklin was becoming more political without even knowing it. He saw that to understand the injustices at Harvard and in the world outside, he would have to learn about politics. He would have to become involved, like his cousin Teddy.

In his sophomore year he helped found a new social club, one that would be open to all students, rich and poor. It had a new name too, a name that suggested how different it was from the Porcellian or the Hasty Pudding: the Harvard Union. Franklin persuaded a family friend to put up the money to buy the building for the Union—a large brick house on Quincy Street—and soon the Union was open for business.

Meanwhile, Franklin became more and more active on the *Crimson.* In 1902, he became one of two assistant managing editors. The next year he was elected managing editor, which meant that he would be the next editor-in-chief, undisputed head of the paper. He was making a success of himself in his own way, a way that did not involve the wealthy society he had come from. He joined the Harvard Political Club and became an active member. He attended meetings in Boston to learn more about how the political system worked. He had been rejected by his own class, but perhaps in the world of politics he would be able to make a place for himself.

At twenty, Franklin was still primarily interested in fitting in. He wanted desperately to be liked. His rejection at Groton and by the Porcellain had given him a sense of identification with the less fortunate in society. Like his cousin, Teddy, Franklin was slowly becoming interested in reform politics. He wanted to learn about the "other half" of society—the immigrants, the workers, the poor. He wanted to know what could be done to make their lives better. This interest in reform was soon sparked even further by an unlikely person, a girl he initially referred to only as "E." He wrote in his diary at the end of his junior year, "E is an angel."

"E" was his cousin, Eleanor Roosevelt, and Franklin had fallen head over heels in love with her.

CHAPTER FIVE

Cousin Eleanor

At first glance, you wouldn't think Eleanor Roosevelt was the kind of girl with whom Franklin would fall in love. Although she had the "right" background, and was even a Roosevelt, she and her cousin were very different.

Franklin was a handsome and outgoing young man. He loved going to parties, dancing the night away with one proper young lady after another. Eleanor, on the other hand, was very shy. She appeared awkward and was generally considered to be "plain." This was not entirely fair. Eleanor had beautiful blonde hair, azure eyes, and a graceful way of moving and speaking. However, she detested her chin, which she said was weak, and despaired over her teeth, which stuck out too much. She believed she was not at all good-looking. An unhappy childhood had not done much to improve her confidence.

While Franklin had been loved and sheltered by his parents, Eleanor's childhood had been insecure and desperately unhappy. Her mother, Anna Hall, had been a great society beauty. Her marriage to Theodore Roosevelt's brother, the dashing Elliott Roosevelt, had been the social event of the season. People said it was a fairytale marriage. But something went wrong. Elliott began drinking too much. By the time little Eleanor was born, the marriage was severely troubled. To make things worse, the beautiful Anna could not hide her disappointment at having such a "plain" daughter. Eleanor sensed her mother's feelings and became an unsmiling, solemn child.

The one love of her young life was her father. He adored her, calling her "his miracle from heaven." But Eleanor's joy in his company was short-lived. His drinking problem was growing worse. More and more he was away from his young family seeking a cure for his drinking in one expensive rest home after another.

Eleanor's mother tried to keep the family together. For a time it looked as if the marriage might have a happy ending, but then tragedy struck. Anna had an operation and died soon afterwards. Elliott, who had been away, returned to take care of Eleanor and her brother. Her father's return filled Eleanor with joy. But Elliott still had too many problems with his drinking. He was simply unfit to care for his children. They were sent off to their Grandmother Hall's house on West 37th Street in New York City. A few months later, Eleanor's beloved father died of a brain tumor.

Grandmother Hall was a hard, bitter woman. The death of her daughter Anna had made her age fast. Now, with this awkward granddaughter to care for, the old woman resorted to stern discipline. Eleanor was made to be a good, obedient child. She was not to be praised or encouraged, but instructed. Years later, a cousin of Eleanor's wrote about the atmosphere of Grandmother Hall's house:

My mother would ask me to go have supper with Eleanor, but I never wanted to go because of the grim atmosphere of that house. There was no place to play games . . . It was not a house for children. The general attitude was "don't do this."

It was a grim place for a sensitive girl to grow up in. Years later Eleanor described her life there as "one long battle against fear." Things improved somewhat when she was sent, at fifteen, to Allenwood, a boarding school in England. For Franklin, boarding school had been a trauma and a disappointment, but for Eleanor it was a liberation. For the first time, she was treated as a worthwhile person. Her keen intelligence soon won her the respect of her teachers and her gentleness won her many friends. Eleanor remembered Allenwood as the happiest time of her life.

She returned to New York City in 1902. She was now seventeen, an elegant young lady. It was time for her to "come out," the expression for the time when young girls from rich families left childhood and entered high society. Eleanor was soon plunged into the rounds of parties, teas, and outings that made up a young debutante's life. But the social whirl was not to Eleanor's taste. The parties made her feel shy and desperate. She tended to stand on the sidelines, watching the prettier girls dancing and flirting. Then something happened that made the situation considerably brighter.

She became friendly with her fifth cousin, Franklin Roosevelt.

Eleanor had always liked Franklin. They had played together as small children, and years later she had met him at a Christmas party when she was thirteen and he was still at Groton.

It was an occasion Eleanor remembered vividly. All the other girls were dressed in long, evening gowns. Meanwhile, Eleanor sat miserably in the corner, wearing a short, "little girl's" dress. She was sure she looked ridiculous. As she feared, no one asked her to dance. She wanted to cry. Suddenly, she heard a voice speaking her name. It was Franklin. Would she dance? He was sixteen and to Eleanor he looked as handsome as a matinee idol in his evening clothes. She never forgot his kindness.

In 1902, she ran into him again by chance, on a train from Washington to New York. It was a hot summer day and the train ride was slow and dull. Franklin was with his mother, Sara. He grew bored and decided to entertain himself by walking through the train. As he entered one of the cars, he saw a girl he thought he knew. It was Eleanor. But this time she was dressed like a young lady in a fine tailored suit. They began to chat. Her sincere way of expressing herself caught Franklin's interest. Would she like to come sit with him and his mother? Eleanor agreed. Under Sara's watchful eye, the two young people continued their conversation. They grew to like each other more and more.

Perhaps because of his own experiences at Groton and Harvard, Franklin was quick to detect Eleanor's shyness and insecurity. It touched him and made him feel at ease with her. When he found his own lightheartedness cheered her up, he grew even more interested in his grave, charming cousin. He discovered that she was like him, informed and interested in the issues of the day. This was new to him in a girl. He found himself telling her about his work on the *Crimson* and his interest in politics. Eleanor told Franklin she felt it was important to do all you could to help right society's wrongs. He asked her what she did to help. Eleanor replied hesitantly that she worked in the slums on the lower East Side of New York, teaching a dancing class to girls and boys at the Rivington Street Settlement. She also helped out at the Children's Aid Society. This sort of activity was unusual in a society girl. Franklin was impressed.

When the train reached New York, Franklin was determined to see more of Eleanor. He began arranging to meet her at parties and dances. Soon his diary was full of notes, such as "Sat next to Eleanor. Very interesting day."

At the beginning of July, he invited Eleanor to Springwood for a house party. Three weeks later he invited her back again. He was falling in love. But his feelings were still a secret. Perhaps he sensed that his mother would not approve. Franklin was careful to act as though Eleanor was merely a close friend. He even arranged to meet her in secret. But, by autumn, his feelings for her could not be hidden. On the weekend of the Harvard-

Yale football game, Franklin asked Eleanor to marry him. She accepted. They were very young—she was barely nineteen and he was just twenty-one—but they were in love and determined to marry.

There was one great obstacle: Franklin's mother, Sara.

Sara had always been protective of Franklin. She had not wanted him to go away to Groton. When he went to Harvard, she had moved to Boston just to be close to him. Since her husband's death, she depended more than ever on her son. Therefore, that Thanksgiving when Franklin at last told her of his plans, Sara was deeply upset.

Marry Eleanor? He was far too young! Although Sara did not say so, she was also puzzled by his choice. Eleanor had always struck her as a rather dull young woman. Surely her son could have found someone more beautiful, more worldly? But Sara was clever enough to keep her objections to herself. She merely said he was awfully young to think of getting married, and that Eleanor was a mere child. At the very least Franklin should keep the engagement secret for a year. Franklin agreed, and Sara decided to use this time to try and prevent the marriage.

That February she invited Franklin and his friend, Lothrop Brown, to join her on a winter cruise around the Caribbean. She hoped that distance would make her son reconsider marrying Eleanor. On board the ship she did her best to interest him in other girls, enlisting Lothrop's help. Nothing worked. Franklin wrote to Eleanor every day. He secretly gave Eleanor several addresses in the Caribbean where she could write to him. Sara's efforts to break them apart gave a romantic urgency to their letters, and when the cruise was over, Franklin returned to New York more determined than ever to marry the woman he had chosen. Sara accepted defeat. Reluctantly, she set about welcoming Eleanor into the family.

The marriage of Franklin and Eleanor Roosevelt was held on Saint Patrick's Day, March 17, 1905. It was the social event of the season. The bride was given away by none other than Theodore Roosevelt, the president of the United States. Franklin's old roommate, Lothrop Brown was best man. The minister was Franklin's old headmaster, Endicott Peabody. Everybody who was anybody in New York society was invited to the festivities.

The bride and groom looked beautiful together. Franklin, in a proper morning suit, made a handsome bridegroom. Eleanor's wedding gown was made of white satin, entirely covered in handmade lace (worn by both her mother and grandmother when they married). A long veil cascaded from her shining blonde hair, held in place by a diamond crescent. Around her neck, she wore Franklin's wedding gift, a gold watch with her initials set in diamonds. But what everyone there commented on was her expression. She looked radiant, they said, as if her face was lit up from inside.

The ceremony took place through the noise of the nearby Saint Patrick's Day parade, passing in the street

Eleanor in bridal pose

outside. Shouts and snatches of music filtered through the open windows. Crowds had gathered outside the house, for word had leaked to the press that the president would be there. Finally, at 3:30 in the afternoon, Franklin and Eleanor were pronounced man and wife.

CHAPTER SIX

An Age of Reform

The early years of the twentieth century were remarkable years for America. The rapid growth of the railroads, mining, steel, oil and other industries had created a prosperous and powerful American upper class. They now had money and time to spend and various diversions and "playthings" on which to spend them. Spectator sports like tennis, horseracing, football and baseball came into vogue. "Playthings" for many wealthy people included a fabulous country home (some even with electric lights) in what quickly became posh resorts. At those resorts, families strolled along manicured paths and rode in their new "horseless carriages," the nickname for early automobiles.

Though the middle class could not afford these things, they could afford to ride bicycles and go to plays, music halls, and the very first movie theaters. Going to the opera was a popular activity, as was getting together informally and singing the popular songs of the day (radios and phonographs were still a few years away from being played at home).

The first years of the twentieth century were filled with hope, discouragement, and public ridicule for two young men named Wilbur and Orville Wright, who were trying to get their heavier-than-air machine to fly. But after December 1, 1903, the brothers would never hear anyone say "Flying is impossible!" again. For on that day, the first airplane flew on its own for a full twelve seconds.

On the ground popular magazines were being eagerly plucked from their shelves in general stores and newsstands. Women were anxious to read the latest advertisements, which had only recently begun to appear in magazines and newspapers.

Advertisers had hit upon this format as a way to tell people about new products. Advertisements for stylish hats appeared, and ads for electric washing machines, with the wash being done in a barrel and the wringing done by hand-crank. Ivory soap ads were first directed at men, calling Ivory a "great shaving soap"; and an ad for an early Oldsmobile compared the cost of feeding a horse ($100 a year) to the cost of gasoline for a year ($35).

Another reason people picked up magazines in those days was to read the latest article exposing yet another scandal in the high ranks of industry and government. The journalists who researched and wrote these stories became known as "muckrakers;" the purpose of these stories was to enlighten the public and to gather support for political and economic reforms.

Such reforms were very much a part of the spirit of this time, which is now called "The Progressive Era." Muckrakers, as well as the small but growing labor unions, were demanding change. Women were beginning to demand voting rights.

The wealthy tended to be quite content with the way

things were, and favored no change at all. For that reason, they generally voted for conservative, Republican presidents. This type of president usually let private business conduct their affairs any way they wanted, without interference from the government. They also relied on the American capitalist system, as well as local charities and governments, to take care of the middle and lower classes. One such politician, Republican William McKinley became president in 1901.

Everything changed when, four months into his administration, President McKinley was shot and killed by a crazed anarchist. Vice-President Theodore Roosevelt, Franklin's cousin, took over as president. The wealthy classes had reason to worry. "Teddy" Roosevelt was an energetic and adventurous man. Though he was born into the ranks of the wealthy, he identified with the common man. His courageous exploits as a soldier were well known, yet he was sensitive to the beauties of nature and literature. This many-sided character led the way for progressive reform—just what the wealthy did not want.

What Theodore Roosevelt aimed for was a "square deal" for both workers and management. He supported labor's demands for a shorter work week and better pay. He also instituted reforms which began to correct the abuses of power in industry and business. Many of the business owners complained loudly at these actions, but the reforms did what Theodore Roosevelt wanted: they helped keep the economy healthy and growing.

Immigrants were coming over to America as never before. The past two decades had brought poor families from England, Ireland, Scandinavia, and Germany in boatloads: the number of yearly immigrants was reaching one million.

Italians, Greeks, and Eastern Europeans, including many Jewish refugees, were arriving daily at New York's Ellis Island. Many were escaping poverty, many were fleeing religious persecution.

As with previous immigrants, the new arrivals competed fiercely for the lowest-paying jobs. A man could work fourteen hours a day as a coal miner and receive fifteen dollars *per month* as his pay. Working conditions continued to be terrible, and the slums the immigrants lived in were filled with garbage, crime, and disease. It is hard today to imagine just how bad their lives were. Yet still they came over. Even those who had been warned about the bad conditions and low pay considered America to be better than what they had at home.

Though at first it seemed that these immigrants only made the labor situation worse, they helped the unions grow. The people from Southern and Eastern Europe had well organized labor unions at home, and their new and strong ideas about union organization added much needed support.

While many foreigners had set their sights on America, America in turn had set its sights on new lands. The ever-expanding American economy reached to find new markets abroad for its goods. Industrialists and investors also wanted to locate new and cheaper outside sources for raw materials. And to a number of Americans, the idea of ruling a foreign country was appealing; this idea of creating a sort of "empire" was called "imperialism."

President Theodore Roosevelt saw that other countries, like Germany, England, France, and Japan were making such "imperialist" and economic claims on small countries in Africa, Latin America, and Asia. Teddy Roosevelt perceived those claims to be a natural outgrowth of any modern and civilized society, and he did not want America to be left out. He wanted to make the United States a world power—to be a strong, well-armed, and active participant in world affairs.

Europe, like America, was sprinting at full speed into the twentieth century. The world was changing faster than at any time in history, perhaps faster than it ever will again. All the countries of Europe were going through the same "growing pains" as was America. The new age set into motion vast and complex events, both at home and abroad, events that would soon sweep up two young, idealistic newlyweds named Franklin and Eleanor Roosevelt.

CHAPTER SEVEN

Growing Pains

By 1905, life for Franklin and Eleanor had settled into a comfortable routine. Franklin passed the bar exam without finishing his law degree at Columbia. He became a law clerk at the New York firm of Carter, Ledyard, and Milburn. Meanwhile, Eleanor was doing her best to be a good housewife. Anna, their first child, was born in May, 1906, and their second, James, a year later. Franklin and Eleanor's life together seemed just about perfect. But below the surface there were tensions, and one great source of tension was Franklin's mother.

Franklin's marriage had not changed Sara Roosevelt's determination to be part of her son's life. Full of energy, she began drawing up plans for two houses to be built side by side on East 66th Street. The houses were to be a Christmas gift for Franklin and Eleanor. Together, mother and son pored over plans for the houses. They excitedly chose wallpaper, carpets, and furniture. They did not consult Eleanor about any of it. Poor Eleanor tried not to mind but she was beginning to feel that she was not in control of her own life. Sara was—and worse, Franklin did not seem to mind.

One day, shortly after the houses were built, Franklin came home from work and found Eleanor in tears. "What on earth is the matter?" he asked. Eleanor burst out with a long list of complaints. She didn't like the house. She didn't like the furniture. In fact, she didn't like anything about it. It did not feel as if it were *hers*. Why should it? Her mother-in-law had taken care of everything! Franklin tried to be sympathetic, but he did not understand. His mother had been very kind to plan the house for them. Couldn't Eleanor see that? Eleanor could not. But she adored her husband, so she dropped the subject and domestic peace was restored—for a time.

In March 1909 she gave birth to her second son. The young couple named him Franklin Delano Roosevelt, Jr. But the baby was sickly, and died of pneumonia when he was barely seven months old. Eleanor was heartbroken. The baby was buried in the Saint James Churchyard in Hyde Park. To Eleanor the churchyard looked terribly cold and somber in October, and she wept bitterly at the thought of leaving her child in such a place. Franklin, young and confused, did his best to comfort her. They both seemed to have so many responsibilities—so much to do and now so many problems.

He was beginning to get tired of his job as a law clerk. The work was interesting on occasion, but Franklin felt the life of a respectable corporate lawyer was not for him. It was too removed from the hustle and bustle of politics. He had not forgotten the goals he had set at Harvard. At heart, he was as committed to them as ever. He began telling other clerks in his law office, "I'm going to be president someday." They almost began laughing, but

Beginning a career in law and politics

he seemed so earnest . . . and, after all, he was a Roosevelt. "With a Roosevelt," the law clerks whispered to
one another, "anything is possible."

But in 1909 it did not seem very likely.

The law firm's clients were people from all walks of
life—businessmen, immigrants, tycoons, and wealthy ladies. They reflected the life of the city, a wild mixture of
types and backgrounds. New York was one of the fastest-
growing and most vital cities in the world. Wall Street
was booming, and every day new businesses were start-

ing up while others went under. It was a time when the ideas of progressivism and reform were sweeping the country. Newspapers and magazines screamed out against all forms of injustice, from political corruption to unsafe canned food.

Franklin felt the excitement he had felt at Harvard. He was becoming more and more convinced that he must get into politics. Franklin despaired at being stuck in his dull law office. Although he did not talk about his plans, he was on the lookout for a way of making his move. Then one day, out of the blue, opportunity came knocking.

John Mack, the district attorney of Duchess County (where Hyde Park was located) told Franklin that the previous state assemblyman, Lewis Stuyvesant Chanler, was retiring. Would Roosevelt be interested in running?

Franklin immediately contacted Tom Leonard, the Democratic chairman for the county. Leonard told him that the town caucus was holding a meeting the next Wednesday night in Poughkeepsie. All the Democratic party bosses in the state would be there. If Franklin was serious about entering politics, he should come to the meeting.

And so at eight o'clock on Wednesday evening, a nervous and eager Franklin Delano Roosevelt presented himself at the town hall in downtown Poughkeepsie. He wore a dark riding habit such as his father might have worn. He looked every inch the young aristocrat. Throughout the first speeches, the men of the caucus studied him. At last, he was formally introduced to the assembly. He stood up and said a few words. He was not yet an experienced politician and his speech was very general, referring vaguely to "reform" and "progress."

The caucus members were not sure he was their man. For one thing, he was too young—only twenty-eight. He was too rich. Would he understand the needs of the district people, workers and farmers? "And what on earth is he wearing?" they murmured to one another. And his glasses! On the other hand, he *was* a Roosevelt. The name alone meant something. More importantly, he was rich. His mother would give him the money for the campaign. At that point, the Democrats in Duchess County did not have much money to put up for the campaign themselves. They discussed Roosevelt's good and bad points among themselves. The caucus members reached a decision: they would give him a try.

Then everything went wrong. Chanler decided not to retire. It would be hopeless to run against Chanler. He was popular and had held the position for years. It looked as if Franklin's political career was over before it had started. But Tom Leonard had an idea. Why didn't Roosevelt run for state senator instead? The incumbent was a Republican, John F. Schlosser. While Schlosser had served several terms and a Democratic victory was unlikely, the campaign would give Franklin valuable experience. Franklin accepted enthusiastically. The campaign was on!

Sara could not get over the change in her boy. In no time he had resigned his "good" job at the law office and was running across the county with all sorts of odd types—politicians, reporters, advisors. The house was full of strange men in rumpled suits. Her son was making speeches everywhere and insisting that everyone call him Franklin! Sara had never liked politics and she did not like this latest turn in her son's career at all. But she might have forgiven everything had it not been for the "Red Peril."

The "Red Peril" was a car—a big, red Maxwell touring car. Richard Connell, the Democratic congressman from New York, lent it to Franklin for his campaign. Richard "Hawkey" Connell was an expert speaker and he accompanied Franklin in a tour of the district he would represent if he were elected state senator. This district, in upstate New York, was 25,000 square miles large, and Franklin toured it all.

In those days cars were not yet being used out in the country. Farmers didn't like them because they scared horses. But they lined up to watch Franklin sitting up in the big, red car as he raced around the countryside with "Hawkey" at the then dangerous speed of twenty-two miles per hour. They wondered who this young man could be, and what he stood for.

Franklin told them. He made speeches everywhere— at roadside taverns, post offices, small general stores, town squares, churches, graveyards, or wherever he saw a few people standing around together alongside the road.

His platform was generally progressive. This meant that he presented himself as being for the common man against big business. In short, he wanted the ordinary worker to get a better deal, and wanted to fight against bosses who mistreated their workers. He would help shopkeepers who had problems getting adequate supplies of goods to sell. He would help farmers compete with large fruit and vegetable merchants. He proposed creating a standard barrel measure—something the farmers had long wanted—to help them control their products against dishonest merchants.

In every speech, he made the same promise. "I will represent you, the people of this district, and no one else. I am pledged to no man, no special interest, and to no boss." This promise was an important part of his campaign, for in those days the political bosses and the boss system were extremely powerful in politics. States, cities, and towns across America had their own "bosses" and these bosses controlled their own political organizations, called "machines."

The boss in New York was a man named William "Boss" Tweed, and his machine was called Tammany Hall after the building where "Boss Tweed" and his cronies met. The Tammany Hall people were Democrats, like Roosevelt, but really they were a party unto themselves. Little happened in New York politics without Boss Tweed's approval. If a bridge needed to be built, for example, building companies would have to pay a bribe to Boss Tweed and his men to get the job. Few officials in New York State were elected to high office without some help from Tammany Hall.

This corruption was tolerated because the boss system sometimes made things more efficient. At that time, city and state governments were under a great deal of strain because of the immigrants who poured into cities and towns. These new Americans needed water, gas, police and firemen—all sorts of city services. The "boss system" helped provide these services quickly. It also made the bosses and their henchmen rich. Of all the bosses in America, Boss Tweed was the most powerful. He ruled over New York State like a dictator.

So, by promising to take on Tammany Hall, Franklin was putting himself out on a limb. He was promising to honestly represent the people, regardless of the desires of Tammany Hall. Voters listened. They were getting fed up with all the corruption, the bribes, and the kickbacks. They were ready for a change. This twenty-eight-year-old Roosevelt seemed to offer it. More and more people across the district began to turn out to listen to the young candidate's speeches.

The Republicans called Franklin a foolish upstart who was putting on a vaudeville show for the farmers. He couldn't possibly expect to win. Newspapers across the state barely mentioned him. He had to pay for his own political ads. The chances were rated five to one against his winning. The Republicans were sure they had nothing to worry about, and that their man, Schlosser, would win once again.

Election Day, November 7, 1910, was cold and gray. Rain was falling as people made their way to the polls. Franklin went back to Hyde Park to wait for the results. The polls opened sluggishly. The rain kept the voters away. In late afternoon, the returns began coming in. No one could believe it. The upstart was not only keeping up with Schlosser, he was beating him! Farmers and voters in small towns across the district had turned out to vote for Franklin. The upstart had won! Franklin Delano Roosevelt, at twenty-eight, was the new state senator from New York. He had defeated his Republican opponent, the "sure winner," by 1,500 votes. He was going to Albany!

CHAPTER EIGHT

Mr. State Senator

O n a sunny cold day in January 1911, twenty-nine-year-old Franklin Delano Roosevelt dashed briskly up the steps of the Albany Statehouse. With his blond hair, handsome face and gold-rimmed spectacles, he looked more like a college student than a state senator. As he entered the assembly room, the other members of the legislature joked about how "green" he looked. Big Tim Sullivan, one of the major "bosses," looked over at Franklin from his seat. "You know those Roosevelts," he called to another Tammany Hall man. "Wouldn't it be safer to drown him before he grows up?" Franklin had not forgotten his campaign promises, and on that cold January morning he was about to begin his first battle against Tammany Hall.

In those days, New York senators to the U.S. Congress were not chosen directly by voters, but by the state legislature. Tammany Hall had just nominated their man. His name was William F. Sheehan, but everyone called him "Blue-eyed Billy." He was a machine politician who had used his influence to make a fortune in trucks and tractors. Now he wanted to be a U.S. senator. Charles F. Murphy, the big boss of Tammany Hall since Boss

Tweed had retired, sent word down that Sheehan was the Democrats' man. Everyone should vote for him.

When Franklin heard about it, he was indignant. He felt that another candidate, Edward Shepard, would make the best senator. Shepard, a lawyer and community leader, believed in honest, progressive government. The bosses were asking—demanding—that all the Democrats in the state assembly vote instead for "Blue-eyed Billy." Franklin was not about to let it happen. *"The Democratic Party is on trial,"* he wrote in his diary.

He joined together with a group of other state assembly members who were unhappy with the bosses. They named themselves the "Insurgents," and vowed to stand against Tammany Hall. They would not vote for Billy Sheehan for Senator no matter what Boss Murphy said.

Murphy threatened not to appoint any of the rebels to any committee positions in the state legislature. Since most important political decisions were made in committees, this was a serious threat. Murphy also said he would not appoint any Insurgents to major jobs in the state political system. Then more assemblymen joined the Insurgents. Franklin was nominated as their chairman, and the "upstart" kid began to speak out for honest government and an end to Tammany Hall. Murphy's threats backfired.

The caucus to nominate the next state senator was held on January 16. Boss Murphy's men got a shock. They did not have enough votes to vote in "Blue-eyed Billy" Sheehan! It looked as if the rebels had won. But

"Boss" Murphy was not leader of Tammany Hall for nothing. As far as he was concerned, the fight was just beginning. He would show Franklin Roosevelt how "real" politics were played. It was an education Franklin never forgot.

Boss Murphy set out to destroy the Insurgents. As Franklin later said, he put "every conceivable form of pressure" on the group. The Insurgents' law firms and businesses were boycotted. State officials they had hired or appointed were fired. Worst of all, Boss Murphy spread evil rumors about them. He told people they were against Billy Sheehan because he was Irish and Catholic.

Franklin was fast learning how unpleasant politics could be. He was also learning how to fight back. He mounted a campaign of his own, speaking out against Boss Murphy whenever he got the chance. Before long, the Insurgents' fight against Tammany Hall was being written up in newspapers across the country. And young Franklin was being praised as a hero. Letters poured into his office from the people who had voted for him. "Good work!" they said. "Stand firm!" These letters made Franklin more determined than ever. The Insurgents were going to win, he told Eleanor confidently.

But he had not learned about politics or politicians. Before long the Insurgents began fighting among themselves. They no longer agreed that Shepard was the best candidate. Moreover, many of them had only gotten involved in the fight for political reasons of their own. Several Insurgents abandoned the group to rejoin the Tammany side. Others tried to take over the group and make it yet another "machine." And of course, Boss Murphy was still in the battle.

Boss Murphy knew how to compromise and he knew how to get what he wanted. Murphy knew the Insurgents were fighting among themselves. He knew that many of them wanted the struggle to end.

In March, Murphy proposed a compromise candidate. His name was Victor Dowling. He was a judge and known to be honest. He was not a strict Tammany man. After a short discussion, the Insurgents agreed to accept him. But the next day when the assembly met to vote on Dowling, they found that his candidacy had been withdrawn. The new candidate—Murphy's choice—was James O'Gorman. He was also a judge and an old Tammany politician. But here was where Murphy's political skill became evident. O'Gorman might be a Tammany politician, but he was also a leader of the Irish community and very, very popular. The Insurgents, still smarting from Murphy's accusations that they were "anti-Irish," could not afford to reject him. As the caucus began, it became clear that the Insurgents were badly divided. After hours of debate, a majority of the group voted to go along with O'Gorman. Only Roosevelt and a few others remained opposed. Boss Murphy had won.

It was Franklin's first taste of how real politics worked. He began to see that politics was not a simple fight of good against evil. There were many different points of view, many different goals and ideals that had to be balanced against one another. Even Tammany Hall was made up of men with different ideas, different personalities. For the first time Franklin began to understand that to be a successful politician—to get things done—one had to be able to compromise. He began to mature. "Politics," he now said, "is the art of the possible." And he was determined to be successful at it.

With the Sheehan fight over, Franklin settled down to day-to-day political life. He built up a "progressive" voting record. He voted for a shorter working week and pushed for a pension plan for retired workers. He supported a bill limiting child labor. He was already becoming interested in national politics.

By election year, one of the presidential candidates particularly interested Franklin. He was the governor of New Jersey, Woodrow Wilson. Wilson was a progressive and a thinker. He had a new vision of America—an America that would work to make liberty and equality real for its citizens. While Wilson was an idealist, he was also an experienced politician. Franklin found his ideas inspiring. He worked for Wilson's campaign in New York. As Franklin moved towards a national stage, Albany reporters began hanging around Franklin's mansion, hoping for a story. He was their favorite "progressive" state senator. One of these "gentlemen of the press," Louis McHenry Howe, was to have a great influence on Franklin's future.

Later called "the man who made the president," Louis Howe was distinguished mainly by his appearance. Howe said of himself that he had "one of the four ugliest faces in the state." Many people agreed. Barely five feet, two inches tall, he wore badly-fitting, stained old suits,

Advisor Louis Howe

and was never seen without a "foul-smelling" cigar in his mouth. He liked to drink. Eleanor disliked the grubby little man on sight. But Franklin saw his valuable qualities. Howe had an uncanny instinct for politics. He knew what got politicians elected. He knew how to get a piece of legislation passed. Franklin recognized that there was plenty Howe could teach him. These men, so unlike one another on the surface, were to become (in the words of Franklin's son, Elliott) "as essential to each other as two parts of a tennis ball—with just one kind of bounce."

Franklin first learned Howe's value shortly after their initial meeting. It was the middle of election year. Franklin was campaigning for re-election to his state senate seat.

One weekend he decided to take a holiday with Eleanor. Together, they set off to Campobello island. When they returned on Sunday they both felt feverish. The doctor was called, and his diagnosis was grim: both had typhoid fever. Franklin panicked. How could he run for office from a sickbed? He remembered Louis Howe. He called him up. Howe, who had recently been fired from his newspaper job, agreed to take over the campaign.

And what a job he did!

Stressing Roosevelt's progressive record, Howe kept Franklin's name in the news—writing brilliant articles aimed at the voters of the district. Howe drove all around the district with his wife, Grace, a large, grim-looking woman who rarely opened her mouth. Howe made speech after speech, tirelessly reminding people what an excellent job State Senator Franklin Roosevelt was doing. Howe's work paid off, for on election day Franklin won by an even larger margin than before.

The results in the national elections were equally exciting. Woodrow Wilson was elected as the president of the United States. Franklin could not get over the news. "Wilson is the man who made me believe in politics again," he told Eleanor eagerly. "His administration will change America." He only wished he could be part of it.

CHAPTER NINE

Mr. Roosevelt Goes to Washington

Franklin had first met Woodrow Wilson in 1911, when he was still governor of New Jersey. Franklin had gone to Wilson to offer to support him for president, and had been impressed with the tall, slim, bespectacled man.

Wilson looked like a professor, but when Franklin spoke to him he realized that Wilson understood politics. Wilson shared his own deepest ideals and beliefs. Wilson believed in reform. He was determined to better the lot of American workers. Wilson's vision was also international. He was a pacifist, and believed that the nations of the world should find peaceful ways to resolve their problems. Now he was running for president. As Franklin sat talking to Wilson in the sunlit, spacious Governor's mansion, he felt his old ideals stir to life again. And now, in November 1912, Woodrow Wilson had been elected the next president of the United States.

Franklin could not help feeling a twinge of regret that he would not be in Washington to see the new administration take charge. He would be stuck in the Albany Statehouse, locking horns with Tammany Hall men like Blue-eyed Billy, Big Tim, and Boss Murphy. The prospect did not thrill him. He thought of trying to line up a position in Washington, but he knew it was unlikely. Then he had a piece of good luck.

He had gone to Washington, D.C. to see Wilson's inauguration on a balmy spring day. The sidewalks along Pennsylvania Avenue were crowded with people who wanted to get a glimpse of their new president. Tired of the crowds, Franklin had stopped in the Willard Hotel to get a cool drink when he ran into Josephus Daniels of North Carolina in the hotel lobby. The two men had met before and had instantly liked each other. Daniels had particularly been impressed with Franklin. He liked his enthusiasm and his stand against Tammany Hall. Daniels had just been appointed secretary of the navy.

"Franklin," Josephus called out. "I have something to talk to you about."

"Yes?" Franklin replied.

"How would you like to come to Washington as assistant secretary of the navy?"

Franklin could hardly believe it. "I'd like it bully well!" he cried. This was perfect! All his life he had loved ships and sailing. He knew about the navy and had studied it for years. The position was tailor-made for him—and, more importantly, he would be in Washington!

Daniels quickly secured approval for Franklin to take on the job.

Franklin frantically prepared to move his family

The young assistant secretary of the navy and his family

down to the capital of the nation. Eleanor was proud of her husband but uneasy about the move. She enjoyed their life in Albany. Besides, the prospect of all the parties and functions she would have to attend as the wife of the new assistant secretary of the navy made her feel positively sick with fear! Although Eleanor was now a busy young mother, at heart she still felt like the shy girl who had stood on the sidelines at dances. Eleanor decided to make the best of it. She found a rambling old townhouse on N Street that belonged to her Aunt Bye. She hired a young woman named Lucy Mercer to be her social sec-

retary. Louis Howe came along as Fr
assistant.

Washington was an exciting place t
form was in the air. Everyone was talki
Freedom"—President Wilson's plan to h
ica a fairer, better country for all its citizen
lin was not directly involved in this, he
who were and listened closely to their id
how national politics worked. He became a
on the Washington social circuit. People li
and vitality. Society wives dubbed him "on
somest men in Washington." In his English -
gold-rimmed, pince-nez glasses, he was the
man on the rise.

Eleanor did not know what to make of h
new popularity. Often she chose to stay ho
went out. Her upbringing had left her with a
too much gaiety. She could not understand
lin saw in all these parties, all these people.
to criticize him for not being "serious" eno
young children to care for she was often tired an
Her husband's love of society was an adde
She wanted to be alone, but he was always dra
out.

They began to quarrel and sometimes did
to each other for days at a time. Eleanor felt that
no longer understood her. There was another
Franklin was becoming close to her social secreta
Mercer. Lucy was a lovely, charming girl, the c
of a Washington society family that had fallen

The young assistant secretary of the navy and his family

down to the capital of the nation. Eleanor was proud of her husband but uneasy about the move. She enjoyed their life in Albany. Besides, the prospect of all the parties and functions she would have to attend as the wife of the new assistant secretary of the navy made her feel positively sick with fear! Although Eleanor was now a busy young mother, at heart she still felt like the shy girl who had stood on the sidelines at dances. Eleanor decided to make the best of it. She found a rambling old townhouse on N Street that belonged to her Aunt Bye. She hired a young woman named Lucy Mercer to be her social secretary. Louis Howe came along as Franklin's personal assistant.

Washington was an exciting place to be in 1912. Reform was in the air. Everyone was talking about "New Freedom"—President Wilson's plan to help make America a fairer, better country for all its citizens. While Franklin was not directly involved in this, he met the people who were and listened closely to their ideas. He learned how national politics worked. He became a popular figure on the Washington social circuit. People liked his charm and vitality. Society wives dubbed him "one of the handsomest men in Washington." In his English-cut suits and gold-rimmed, pince-nez glasses, he was the perfect young man on the rise.

Eleanor did not know what to make of her husband's new popularity. Often she chose to stay home while he went out. Her upbringing had left her with a mistrust of too much gaiety. She could not understand what Franklin saw in all these parties, all these people. She began to criticize him for not being "serious" enough. With young children to care for she was often tired and anxious. Her husband's love of society was an added burden. She wanted to be alone, but he was always dragging her out.

They began to quarrel and sometimes did not speak to each other for days at a time. Eleanor felt that Franklin no longer understood her. There was another problem: Franklin was becoming close to her social secretary, Lucy Mercer. Lucy was a lovely, charming girl, the daughter of a Washington society family that had fallen on hard times. She had shining hair, warm, dancing eyes, and a voice that was described as "dark velvet." Unlike Eleanor, she enjoyed socializing and Franklin often took her along to parties and dinners in Eleanor's place. Eleanor tried not to get jealous. But with small children, she felt she was a poor rival to the lovely young Lucy. In her insecurity, Eleanor withdrew further from Franklin. Sadly, as both would admit years later, it was then that the gulf between them began to widen, until their lives were quite separate.

Despite the difficulties in his home life, Franklin loved his new job and took to it like a duck to water. Franklin and his new boss, Josephus Daniels, could not have been more different. While Franklin had the looks and manners of a young aristocrat, Josephus looked more like an old country preacher. His face was rough-hewn. He wore dusty black suits and old-fashioned string ties. He was a slow-moving, cautious man while Franklin, especially in his new job, was definitely not.

Franklin's old love of ships and sailing re-emerged. He became a passionate supporter of a powerful navy. Daniels, too, believed in a strong navy—but not to the extent that Franklin did. Franklin flung himself into the task of building up America's naval forces like a whirlwind. He toured shipyards. He spoke with admirals, battleship commanders, sailors, and shipbuilders. He also frequently criticized Daniels for moving too slowly. The two were soon in opposition, and many people in Washington said that if Daniels had not had the patience of a saint, he would have fired his brash assistant secretary.

But Daniels recognized Franklin's worth. Besides, the navy men loved him. Franklin knew ships and he knew naval strategy. They wished secretly that he, and not Daniels, were their commander.

Although Daniels moved too slowly for Franklin's taste, he knew how to deal with Congress where Franklin did not. He watched admiringly as Daniels persuaded senators and congressmen to devote funds for new ships. Daniels knew how to speak to Congress; he knew how to use facts and figures to argue his case. He also knew how to compromise. Slowly, Franklin grew to respect his superior. He might not be supportive enough of the navy, but he was good at politics. Franklin was learning once again the importance of the art of politics.

It was a lesson Franklin seemed to forget in the spring of 1914. Despite the pleas of both Louis Howe and Josephus Daniels, Franklin decided to take on a new challenge: he would enter the race for senator of New York. It was not a bad idea on the surface. Franklin was well connected in Washington, and had solid political experience behind him. But he forgot one thing: he had been away from New York State for over two years. He announced a progressive, "anti-boss" platform. Once again he underestimated "Boss" Murphy.

Murphy had a long memory. He had not forgotten his fight with Franklin. Now he planned to defeat him again. His plan for doing it was simple and effective. Franklin was counting on President Wilson's complete support of his campaign. Without it, Franklin was lost.

So Murphy came up with a way of taking it from him. The Tammany candidate would be an even stronger Wilson man than Franklin: Wilson's ambassador to Germany, James Gerard.

Gerard was a personal friend of Wilson's. Like Franklin, he was in favor of reform. Boss Murphy informed Wilson that support of Franklin Roosevelt, a candidate who had "irresponsibly attacked and defamed members of the New York State government," would cause serious problems. "It will divide the party," Murphy told President Wilson. Wilson knew what that meant. Tammany Hall men would vote against him in Congress and in the Senate. In order to pass the laws that made up his "New Freedom" plan, Wilson needed all the Democrats to vote together. As much as Wilson liked Franklin, he could not risk his relationship with the Congress. Quietly, Wilson downplayed his support for Franklin's campaign. On November 7, 1914, Franklin suffered his first defeat at the polls.

The defeat hurt—a lot. But Franklin had learned his lesson once and for all. To be a successful politician, you have to make compromises. You must work with people, even when you disagree with them. He might not like the men of Tammany Hall, but he would never get elected without them. He had to learn to work with men like Big Tim Sullivan and Boss Murphy. He had to learn how to get them to do what he wanted.

It was a lesson that would serve Franklin well in the next couple of years, for as soon as he had recovered from his campaign loss, he was called back to Washington. Woodrow Wilson had been elected to a second term as president. Franklin was needed in his old job. Ominous events were unfolding in Europe, and wise men spoke of war on the horizon.

CHAPTER TEN

A Navy Man

The countries of Europe had been moving toward open conflict for some time. There had been fights over colonies, over trade, and over borders. Three international conferences failed to resolve the problems. Tension was mounting. Then on July 28, 1914, in the tiny country of Serbia, the Austro-Hungarian Archduke Ferdinand was assassinated. The tensions of Europe exploded into World War I.

Austria-Hungary declared war on Serbia. Germany joined the fight on the Austro-Hungarian side. Russia and France jumped in to protect Serbia. On August 1, Germany declared war on Russia and France and immediately invaded neutral Belgium, bringing England into the war.

America responded with horror and disgust. President Wilson was a pacifist, and in 1914 many Americans agreed with him. War has always been a terrible waste of lives, but modern warfare—with machine guns, poison gas, and tanks—is especially tragic. America was determined to stay out of it. On August 4, President Wilson declared:

"The United States must be neutral in fact as well as in name . . . impartial in thought as well as in action."

69

As the war in Europe spread, America tried to do just that. But some people saw early on that eventually America would have to get involved. In a war as big as this, it was impossible to stay neutral. One of those people was Franklin Delano Roosevelt.

He was a Navy man and grasped right away the effect of the war on an issue vital to American interests: freedom of the seas.

The United States had extensive trade with all the countries of Europe, and especially England. To have any chance of winning the war, England was forced to put a tight naval blockade around Germany. Any ships bearing goods to Germany would be seized and their cargoes confiscated. This was against the principle of freedom of the seas which America had once fought to defend. But the English were eager to keep America's goodwill. Therefore, they kept sea lanes to Europe open for American ships (as long as they weren't going to Germany). They also put in huge orders for American food and goods. Despite the blockade, the relationship between America and England remained friendly. This was not the case, however, with America and Germany.

In February 1915, the German kaiser retaliated for the British blockade by announcing that all waters around the British Isles were now a "war zone." *Any ship of any nationality* that tried to trade with England, France, or any of the Allies, would be destroyed by German submarines or U-boats, as they were called. The Americans responded angrily. The kaiser's announcement made it impossible for America to trade with Europe! But the German government refused to back down. Relations between the two countries were growing tense. Then on May 7, 1915, a German U-boat torpedoed and sank the *Lusitania*, a cruise ship sailing off the coast of Ireland. No soldiers were aboard, only innocent vacationers. Eleven hundred civilians were drowned in the icy waters, including 128 Americans. The Germans made no attempt to rescue the passengers. This cold-blooded act of war enraged the American public. Anti-German sentiment quickly rose. The German government still refused to give in to American demands for free passage of their ships. It was only a matter of time before the two countries declared war.

Franklin saw America's entry into the war coming. The Navy, he felt, had to be prepared for war. But many in the department, including his boss, Josephus Daniels, did not see it his way. They still hoped for peace. Impatient, Franklin set about doing what needed to be done, ignoring rules and regulations. Many years later, Franklin said that he broke so many laws during this period, he should have gone to jail for nine hundred and ninety-nine years! At the time, he did not care. Nothing was important except preparing the navy for the coming battle.

After President Wilson's re-election in 1916, relations between America and Germany rapidly declined. On January 30, 1917, the German government announced that they would begin "unrestricted" submarine warfare. This meant that any neutral ships—especially American ships—would be sunk on sight if they entered waters around the British Isles. Two days later America broke

diplomatic relations with Germany. On April 6, a sad-
dened President Wilson called a special session of Congress to declare war on Germany. Never has a President
declared war more reluctantly than Wilson.

> It is a fearful thing to lead this great, peaceful people
> into war, into the most terrible and disastrous of all wars.
> But the right is more precious than peace, and we shall
> fight for the things we have always carried nearest our
> hearts—for democracy.

He now understood, as had Franklin Roosevelt, that
America could not stay out of the conflict any longer.

Now that war had begun, Franklin was busier than
ever—inspecting ships, ordering weapons and supplies,
recruiting sailors, and planning strategy. It was an enormous job, but very quickly America was working full
steam to win the war.

What American soldiers saw convinced them once
again of the importance of peace. The battles across Europe had been brutal. The new technology of weapons
had made it the deadliest war in history. In France, England, and Germany an entire generation of young men
were lost to the battle trenches. Europeans were tired and
bitter. The war had made them feel that they had destroyed their civilization, and that what had taken its place
was barbaric and harsh. In January 1918, President Wilson
announced his "Fourteen Points" plan for maintaining
peace once war was over. It was clear the Allies would
win eventually, but Wilson was determined to make sure

that such a war never happened again. With his Fourteen Points, he tried to set rules that would allow the nations of Europe to live together in harmony. The last point of the fourteen, the one closest to Wilson's heart, called for the formation of a League of Nations. Here, countries of the world would solve their conflicts through argument and negotiation—not war. Wilson hoped to construct a new and better world from the ashes of the World War.

While Wilson was thinking of the problems of peace, his young assistant secretary of the navy was busy thinking about war. Franklin had always worshiped his cousin, Theodore Roosevelt, as a hero. During the Spanish-American War, Theodore Roosevelt had commanded the legendary "Rough Riders." He had been a soldier. What was he, Franklin, doing behind a desk at a time like this? He should be on a ship, bravely serving his country. In June 1918, he pleaded with President Wilson and Josephus Daniels to let him resign his cabinet post, so he could take a commission. Both Daniels and Wilson refused. Franklin was far too valuable where he was. Besides, was he so sure he wanted to be in the thick of battle? Did he know what war was really like?

Franklin was not convinced. He wanted to be near the front lines. At last, in July of 1918, he got his wish. Wilson sent him on an official trip to examine Navy bases and meet with the leaders of the European Allies. For Franklin it was like an adventure book come to life. He set out, speeding across the Atlantic in a naval destroyer, recklessly skirting war zones, coming perilously close to battle. He toured naval bases across Europe. He lived with sailors and soldiers. He examined weapons, and came under artillery fire on several occasions. He saw mass graves of young soldiers who had given up their lives. He saw men younger than him whose lungs had been ruined by the poisonous "mustard" gas used in the trenches and scores of others who had been crippled by gunshot, mines, and torpedoes. He would never stop secretly longing to be a real navy man, but Franklin understood now how costly war could be. For the first time, he began to appreciate Woodrow Wilson's commitment to lasting peace.

In November 1918, the "War to End All Wars" at last came to a finish. For the first time in five years the guns were silent. Sad-faced, exhausted soldiers returned home. It was a victory without joy. The war had been too costly. The new machines of war had been too efficient—hundreds of thousands of young men lay dead on the fields of Verdun, Argonne, and Ypres. This was death on a scale unknown before.

Now came the difficult job of constructing a peace settlement. The peace conference was held in January 1919, in the fabulous palace of Versailles just outside Paris. President Wilson and the Americans set out with high hopes. They were certain that after such a terrible war, Europe would be only too glad to adopt a solid plan for lasting peace. It quickly became apparent that their European allies had other ideas. They wanted revenge on Germany for starting the war. The Treaty of Versailles reflected this. Germany lost territory, and the German people were forced to pay back the Allies for the damage they had done. The peace conference was full of fighting and disputes. Wilson looked on sadly. The war had been hard, and peace was bitter. Woodrow Wilson's Fourteen Points meant nothing to the combative rulers of Europe. Surprisingly, nation after nation voiced their support for one point of the plan, Wilson's idea for a "League of Nations." Despite his disappointment over the Treaty of Versailles, Wilson returned to America in triumph. The League of Nations had the support of people around the world. It looked as if Wilson's dream of a lasting peace would soon become a reality.

As the president's ship drew into Boston harbor, the huge crowd that had come to meet it burst into wild cheers. Wilson was returning home a hero. On the deck beside Wilson stood another convert to the dream of the League of Nations, Franklin Delano Roosevelt. He had attended the conference with Eleanor. After watching his president eloquently plead the cause of peace with the leaders of Europe, he had become convinced that Wilson was right. The cost of war was far too high, the rewards far too low. The people of the world needed to find a way to live together peacefully. The League of Nations was the best way of doing that. And he, Franklin Roosevelt, would do all he could to see that the American people voted for it.

CHAPTER ELEVEN

Dreams and Defeat

In the spring of 1919 Franklin set about helping Wilson campaign for the League of Nations. He was eager and excited, and gave speeches around the country in favor of the League. He compared it to the American Constitution. "It may not end wars," he said, "but nations demand the experiment."

The American people were not interested. They were tired of war, tired of the problems of Europe. They had lost fathers, brothers, sons, and husbands. They were worn out and wanted to return to problems of their own. Prices had been going up. Troubles between workers and management were mounting. Why should Americans worry about the League of Nations? Times had changed since the "progressive" years before the war. People's ideas had changed too.

Franklin was puzzled by America's indifference to the League. President Wilson was heartbroken. His speeches grew more passionate about the need for the League, the need to prevent war. Few wanted to listen. Exhausted by his efforts, Wilson collapsed during a speech in Pueblo, Colorado on September 25, 1919. He was rushed back to Washington. But it was too late. A blood clot had left him paralyzed and near death. Although he regained consciousness, Wilson was never to fully recover.

For Franklin, Wilson's collapse was another harsh lesson in the art of politics. Franklin saw once again that a politician must always pay attention to what the voters need and want—not what the politician *thinks* they need and want. Wilson had poured his life into fighting for the League of Nations. It was his dream. It was a good dream, but it had not been the right time to present it to the American people. The fight had left Wilson a broken man. In the summer of 1920, Franklin set out for the Democratic Convention determined to make a final pitch for the League of Nations in Wilson's honor.

The convention was held in San Francisco. Despite the warm July weather, the politicians gathered there were not feeling very cheerful. Their president lay sick in the White House. The mood of the country was turning against them. Worst of all, they had no candidate to take the place of Woodrow Wilson.

The convention was noisy and active. Delegates circled the convention floor, putting up names for nomination and trying to get votes for their favorite candidates. Twenty-two names were put up for nomination—a huge number. Franklin gave the nominating speech for his favorite candidate, Alfred E. Smith, a "progressive" politician from his home state of New York. But Al Smith, a man who had risen to political prominence from the tough streets of New York City did not have much

77

chance of winning. The real race was between three men: William McAdoo of California, A. Mitchell Palmer of Pennsylvania, and Governor James M. Cox of Ohio. McAdoo was President Wilson's son-in-law, and very popular. As the convention wore on, the tide turned against him. He was too close to Wilson, many delegates said. People were tired of Wilson and his League. It was time for the Democrats to try something new. They finally settled on a "compromise" candidate, James M. Cox of Ohio.

Cox was an experienced politician. He was more practical, less idealistic than Wilson. However, the Democrats needed a vice-presidential candidate more like Wilson to balance the ticket. Cox, by himself, was not charismatic enough to sway voters. They needed someone who would reflect the old ideals of the party. They needed a "Wilson man." Names were proposed and rejected. Cox suggested young Franklin Roosevelt. His name was put up and voted on. "Yes" votes poured in. Roosevelt was swept onto the ticket. At thirty-eight, Franklin was running for the second highest office in the land!

Franklin rose to the podium to accept the nomination. He dedicated himself to world peace and to the League of Nations. "The good, old days are gone past forever; we have no regrets," he began, "for our eyes are trained ahead—forward, to better new days. America's opportunity is at hand. We can lead the world by great example."

The campaign began. Franklin tirelessly crisscrossed the country, campaigning for James Cox. He made speeches, gave tours, and mingled with the voters. Although he sensed people were not interested, he stuck desperately to the dream of the League of Nations. It was the least he could do for Wilson. But even he was forced to recognize the country was not with them.

It was a hard campaign. Franklin traveled endlessly. Louis Howe and Eleanor came with him. Eleanor had always disliked Howe, but during this campaign she came to see how much he knew about politics and, more importantly, how devoted he was to Franklin. For his part, Louis Howe saw how well Eleanor took to politics. She seemed to have a flair for it, he told his boss. She understood the issues. What was more, she *felt* for the voters. She had a knack for saying what was on their minds. As the trip wore on, Howe involved her more and more in the inner workings of the campaign. Both he and Franklin began to rely on her advice. Franklin and Eleanor's marriage had been through severe storms, but now, despite their personal differences, the two worked together as a team.

Their work was for nothing. The country had indeed turned away from the Democrats. On November 2, the Republican candidate, Warren G. Harding, won by one of the biggest landslides in American history. In his acceptance speech, Harding declared "America's present need is not heroics, but healing; not revolution, but restoration." For Franklin these words seemed to confirm that the ideals of reform and progress, the goals he had fought for, were out of fashion, and would be for some time. Sadly, he watched as Woodrow Wilson left the White House on inauguration day, a sick and broken man.

This was a difficult period of Franklin Roosevelt's life. There was no role for him in politics now. He went into business and invested in a wide range of companies. But at heart he was no businessman. He missed the action and excitement of politics. It was a quiet time in his life, he told friends. But Franklin did not much like being quiet. He was already thinking of the future with his typical optimism. "The moment of defeat," he wrote to a friend, "is the best time to plan for victory." Then something happened to upset all his plans.

It began one warm August morning in 1921. Franklin, Eleanor, and all their children were on vacation in Campobello. Franklin and the children had gone fishing aboard a friend's yacht, the *Sabalo*. As the boat drew out over the cool water, Franklin made everyone laugh by dashing back and forth across the deck of the boat, baiting hooks, and giving advice. He lost his footing and slipped. A cry went up. Franklin had fallen overboard! He was soon fished out, but everyone noticed how gray he looked. The water had been awfully cold, so cold it had shocked him. "I never felt anything so cold as that water," he said later. "It seemed paralyzing."

The chill of the water seemed to cling to him, but he ignored it.

The next day, his arms and legs ached. He spotted a forest fire blazing on a nearby island. A fire was everyone's business! Franklin summoned his sons James, Elliott, and Franklin. Together they sailed over to help fight

Fire at island near Campobello

it. Once there, they spent hours beating down the hissing flames with damp clothes and pine branches. It was late afternoon before the fire was finally put out. Franklin and his sons were covered in soot and ash, exhausted, their eyes smarting from the smoke. Ever cheerful, Franklin proposed a swim. The children agreed enthusiastically. When the swim was over, Franklin could not stop shivering. "I think I'll go to bed without any supper tonight," he announced. "I musn't catch a cold." He was supposed to take the children camping the next day and didn't want to get sick and ruin the trip.

Franklin expected that he would be his old self after a night of rest. But the next morning when Eleanor came in to see him his fever was 103 degrees. The trip would have to be postponed. The Howes were visiting, and Louis's wife, Grace, was happy to lead the camping trip. A quiet house was just what Franklin needed to recover from his "flu."

Once the children were gone, Eleanor tried to make Franklin comfortable. All through the morning, his fever remained high. He began complaining of terrible stabbing pains in his legs and back. Eleanor called Louis Howe to come up and look at him. Howe did not like what he saw. His boss was flushed and clearly in pain. Howe said they should call a doctor immediately.

Campobello was very isolated. The Roosevelts did not even have a telephone. Eleanor managed to get word to the mainland. That evening the local doctor, an old country physician named Bennet, came over in his row-boat. He examined the patient. Franklin's fever was high, but Dr. Bennet was sure it was nothing more than a bad cold. "Make sure the patient gets plenty of rest and give him lots of fluids to drink," Dr. Bennet told Eleanor before he rowed back.

Louis Howe and Eleanor looked at each other. They wanted to believe it was just a cold, as the doctor said. But the two of them felt uneasy. Neither had ever seen a cold like this. That night the children returned early from their camping trip. They all had the same symptoms as their father. They complained of stiff necks and aches in their arms and legs. Eleanor had a whole family to nurse. By the next morning the children were better. Franklin was not. On the morning of August 12, he tried to get out of bed and fell down. By afternoon, he was almost completely paralyzed.

CHAPTER TWELVE

Dark Days

The next few weeks were the hardest of Franklin's life. His condition grew dramatically worse. His legs were now in such terrible pain that even the weight of the bed sheet was a torture. The muscles of his face were paralyzed. He could barely speak. In a panic, Eleanor summoned Dr. Bennet back. The old country doctor could not explain why a "simple cold" would have such an effect. Franklin was now so sick it was impossible to move him. Louis Howe set off on a desperate search for a specialist—a doctor who could help Franklin.

He went to Eastport, the nearest town. He found a Philadelphia surgeon named Keen who was willing to make the trip to the island. Keen struck Louis as opinionated and pompous, but he was the best they could do. He was rushed to Franklin's bedside. Keen quickly made his diagnosis: a blood clot had settled on Franklin's lower spine. It had caused a temporary paralysis, and with constant massages the patient would soon be better. Eleanor and Louis were told to begin massaging the patient immediately. So they did. Eleanor and Louis took turns, stopping only to catch a few hours of sleep. The massages were agony to Franklin. Every touch brought new and sharper pain to his tortured limbs. Franklin bore it bravely. He would be better soon. Despite all Eleanor and Louis's careful nursing, there was no improvement.

Dr. Keen was called back. He now concluded that Franklin must have a lesion of the spine. Eleanor and Louis were to keep up the treatment. Franklin was weakening. Eleanor did not know what to do. Sick with worry, Louis sent a letter to Franklin's uncle, Fred Delano, describing the illness in detail. Fred Delano was a hardheaded, sensible businessman. He realized that something serious was the matter. He took the letter directly to Dr. Robert Lovett, a well-known specialist in Boston. Without even seeing Franklin, Dr. Lovett made a firm diagnosis: this was poliomyelitis. There could be no mistake. Franklin had polio.

In those days polio was a terrifying and mysterious disease. There had been epidemics of it for several years, but no one knew just what it was or what caused it. Polio usually struck young children; most of its victims were infants under five. It attacked the nervous system. Aside from strict quarantines of polio victims, no one knew how to stop or cure polio. Franklin's was a highly unusual case. Not many healthy adult men had fallen victim to polio. This helps explain why it had taken so long to diagnose his case, but it did not explain what the Roosevelts should do now. Louis and Eleanor were frightened. How would they tell Franklin? How would an energetic, ambitious man like Franklin adjust to being a cripple in a wheelchair perhaps for life?

Dr. Lovett ordered Eleanor to stop the massages im-

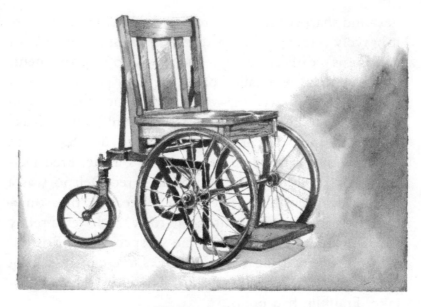

F.D.R.'s wheelchair

mediately. They might harm Franklin's damaged muscles and nerves even further. For the time being, the patient must simply rest and wait. Later, he could begin a program of physical therapy.

The next month passed slowly. When the illness had passed, Franklin was still in agony. He regained use of his facial muscles, but his arms were still weak, and it was difficult to move them. His legs could not move. He could not sit up. He could not write, or even turn the pages of a book. On the surface he seemed cheerful. When his frightened children were brought to the doorway to see him, he always managed a joke, a smile, or a nod. Inside, he felt depressed and empty. What kind of future would he have now? He wondered if he would be an invalid for life. The idea was intolerable to him.

Eleanor and Louis watched over him anxiously. They could sense his despair, however hard he fought to conceal it. They tried to keep his spirits up, but they, too, often felt the hopelessness of the situation. They also had a decision to make. Should they announce Franklin's illness, or try to keep it a secret?

It was a more important decision than it seemed. Both Louis and Eleanor knew that if word slipped out that Franklin Delano Roosevelt had polio, his career in politics might well be over. No one would take him seriously as a candidate, especially if they knew how serious it was. Losing his career in politics would destroy Franklin, who was already depressed. Eleanor and Louis decided that the illness must be kept secret. Not even Franklin's mother, Sara, who was away in Europe, was told. The children were not told. And Louis leaked to the press only that Franklin was suffering from a "serious flu" and was expected to recover shortly.

August ended. Cool breezes drifted across the island. Eleanor and Louis continued to nurse their patient. Sara Roosevelt, who had been told about Franklin's illness upon her return, rushed to join them. As the leaves on the trees across Campobello changed color, the three decided that Franklin was at last well enough to be moved to a hospital in New York. The move was planned in detail by Louis Howe. Although Franklin could not even sit upright, Louis Howe, ever the political mastermind, was determined that Franklin should not seem broken or defeated. Despite his illness, he was to be the same old "gallant" Roosevelt everyone knew.

Fred Delano arranged for a private railroad car to wait for Franklin across the bay in Eastport. Louis knew the press would be waiting, so he leaked to reporters that Franklin would not be landing at Eastport as expected but on a distant dock, ten miles out of town. This would give the Roosevelts time to get Franklin ashore and settled before the reporters and well-wishers found him. Thus, the first image the world had of Franklin Delano Roosevelt after his illness was that of a feisty patient propped up in a stretcher inside a railroad car. Franklin was wearing his favorite fedora tilted back jauntily. In his hand he held a cigarette. His large body was limp, but his face and his mannerisms were the same as they had always been. Franklin's voice was firm, his smile wide and dazzling. He told reporters with a lighthearted laugh, "I am feeling much, much better." He said it with such conviction that few of the onlookers had any trouble believing that the vital man in front of them would be up and about in no time. Only Louis and Eleanor wondered what, if anything, Franklin's future would hold. They both knew how important the dream of being in politics was to him. How would he achieve a place in politics now?

The train pulled away from Eastport Station. Franklin was on his way to Presbyterian Hospital in New York. His new doctor, George Draper, was an old Harvard

Train to hospital

friend. The worst part of the disease was over. Franklin's spirits began to rise. Many victims of polio walked and led active lives again. Surely it was only a matter of time before he was back to normal again. He was going to recover. He was going to walk.

CHAPTER THIRTEEN

The Road Back

When Franklin entered Presbyterian Hospital in New York City, Louis Howe at last released the story of his illness to the papers. Howe quoted the doctors that "there would be no permanent injury from the attack." In other words, Franklin would not be left a cripple. It was an optimism Franklin shared. "I expect to leave in two or three weeks on crutches," he told friends.

Although Franklin was released from the hospital in six weeks, there was no real improvement in his legs. He threw himself into a strenuous physical exercise program. He trained himself to crawl by pulling himself along with his arms. He exercised his upper body until, as he reported proudly, he had "muscles Jack Dempsey (the famous boxer) would envy." His legs remained paralyzed. Muscles in his legs were weak; he could not keep them straight unless he wore heavy metal braces which were painful and uncomfortable. Franklin remained convinced that he would find a cure. It was only a matter of months before he would learn to walk again.

The cure that attracted him the most was water. "The water," he often said, "put me where I am, and the water has to bring me back." Swimming, his doctor told him, particularly in warm waters, was the best possible therapy for people crippled by polio. In the spring of 1923, Franklin bought himself a houseboat. He named it the *Lorooco*, and it soon became a second home.

Every winter, he would sail for Florida with a party of family and friends. Franklin explored the Florida coast, stopping at deserted white beaches and abandoned coves. He would swim every day for hours at a time. At each stroke of his powerful arms, he felt hopeful. His atrophied limbs seemed to come alive in the water, and sometimes he felt as if his legs could once again carry him. When he wasn't swimming, he fished or played cards. It was a relaxing routine, and Franklin soon looked healthier than he had in years. His face was tanned now and his smile was dazzling. Eleanor was becoming seriously involved in politics now and was often away. Franklin's constant companion in Florida was his new secretary, Missy LeHand. Missy was a cheerful woman with a vibrant smile. Like Louis Howe, she was to dedicate her life to working for Franklin. Years later, she described him as the most magnetic personality she had ever known. Aboard the *Lorooco* she took good care of him. She encouraged him in his program of exercise. Missy was sure that it was only a matter of time before her boss strode through the convention halls as he once had.

It was a quiet, disciplined life, so different from politics, but one that Franklin soon grew to love. His health and his confidence improved steadily. The warm waters were working, he told friends exuberantly. He would soon be able to walk again. Then he would return to politics.

In April 1924, however, politics called on him.

His old friend, Al Smith, was running for president. He called Franklin up. Would Franklin head the "Al Smith for President" committee in New York State? Franklin hesitated. His strength had improved, but he still could not move his legs. The Florida water might work if he gave it more time. On the other hand, if he refused this opportunity, would he ever get another chance? He argued back and forth with himself.

He accepted Smith's offer. Franklin rejoined political life with all his old enthusiasm and flair. With the help of Louis Howe, he was soon busy trying to drum up support for Smith everywhere he could. He did such a good job that Smith asked him yet another favor. Would Franklin make the speech nominating him for president at the Democratic Convention?

This was a real challenge. Franklin thought long and hard about it. He had not given a major speech since 1920, before he had been crippled by polio. Could he stand before all the party members and leaders and speak? He was slowly learning to support himself using his powerful arm and chest muscles, but there was still a chance he might not be able to stand at all. If he was going to give the speech, he was going to do it standing. Could he? Franklin told Al Smith that he would make the speech.

In June 1924, the Democrats assembled in the smoke-filled hall of New York's Madison Square Garden. Franklin arrived in a wheelchair with his son, James. In his arms he held a pair of crutches.

As in 1920, the Democratic party was in bad shape. The Republicans still occupied the White House. Calvin Coolidge, the Republican candidate, was popular with the voters. He was a New Englander who never said a word unless he absolutely had to. The voters saw him as a good, steady man. America was doing well. The stock market was booming. Industry was expanding. No one saw the need for change. The Republican party seemed to bring with it prosperity. The Democrats were divided among themselves, uncertain of what they stood for. It was not the Democrats' year. At Madison Square Garden the mood was gloomy and strained. Even so, an excited hush fell over the room as Franklin Delano Roosevelt's name was called to step forward to the speaker's platform.

Heads turned as James Roosevelt snapped his father's leg braces into place. James pulled him to his feet. Franklin tucked his crutches under his arms and, slowly but steadily, walked to the great platform with his son beside him. The crowd had fallen silent. Franklin handed his crutches to his son and, supporting himself, began to speak. His voice was strong and deliberate. His words carried to all parts of the huge hall. His speech recalled the ideals of the Democratic party—referring to their history of reform, of progress. Franklin praised Al Smith as the man who could make this history—the dreams and ideals of the party—come alive again. Al Smith, he said, "has a personality that carries to every bearer not only the sincerity, but the righteousness of what he says. He

93

F.D.R. continues politics on crutches

is the 'Happy Warrior' of the political battlefield." For a moment, the hall was as still as a church. Then the crowd burst into wild applause. Many held back tears at the sight of Franklin standing straight and strong before them. The phrase "Happy Warrior," which Franklin had used to describe Al Smith, became etched in people's minds as a description of Franklin himself. Everyone could see the braces on his legs. Everyone knew how serious his illness had been. As far as they were concerned, he had beaten it. He looked like a "warrior," a "happy warrior" in the arena of national politics, and for the first time, many party members saw him as a future leader.

No speech, no matter how good, could save the Democrats that year. Despite Roosevelt's stirring nomination of Al Smith, the convention was soon deadlocked. In the end, a compromise candidate, a lawyer from West Virginia named John W. Davis, was chosen. The Democrats knew he had no chance of winning. While the convention had been a loss for the Democratic party, for Franklin it had been a triumph. He had met the challenge. He could again be a force in politics.

A second event lifted Franklin's spirits. George Peabody, a philanthropist, had writtten to him about a natural mineral spring in the Georgia countryside. The place was called Warm Springs, and Peabody wrote that the waters had miraculous healing powers. Franklin should try them for his polio. Franklin had always believed that water would cure him. Even the name of the place filled him with hope. He would go to Warm Springs. The next Democratic Convention was four years away and Franklin wanted to enter it walking!

CHAPTER FOURTEEN

Warm Springs

When Franklin, Eleanor, and Missy first set sight on Warm Springs in October of 1924, it did not look like the ideal spot for a "miracle cure." Warm Springs had once been a popular resort, but now it was desolate and forlorn looking. The hotel and cottages around the spring were near ruin. The large hotel was ramshackle, with peeling paint and dusty, cracked windows. The cottages were in even worse condition. Their walls were buckling. The roofs leaked. Franklin did not let appearances discourage him. Franklin proposed that they give the famous "spring" a try. After that first swim, Franklin was a convert to the "magic waters." The spring would cure him! He felt sure of it.

The underground spring flowed into a huge natural pool from nearby Pine Mountain. The water, heated by the rocks beneath, maintained a constant temperature of 88 degrees. Yet perhaps because of all the minerals it contained, it was not tiring to bathe in. On the contrary, the water seemed to give all who swam in it a feeling of health and well-being. The action of the spring kept the water in the pool constantly agitated, so that it "massaged" the swimmer. It was just the thing for his paralyzed legs,

F.D.R. swimming at Warm Springs

Franklin reported enthusiastically. Even after one swim, the three of them felt better, more alive.

From then on, Franklin spent most of his time at Warm Springs. He was eventually to put over two thirds of his private fortune into purchasing and repairing the resort.

He struck up a friendship with the manager of the hotel, a tall, gentle Southerner named Tom Loyless. Together, Tom and Franklin planned to turn the place into a therapeutic center for polio victims. Louis Howe, always interested in keeping his boss in the public eye, released an item about Franklin to the newspapers. "FRANKLIN DELANO ROOSEVELT WILL SWIM

HIS WAY TO HEALTH," headlines across the country trumpeted. The story beneath gushed about the "miracle effects" of the warm spring. Within months, polio victims were streaming to the resort. It was time for the Warm Springs therapeutic center to open its doors.

Franklin soon found himself in a new role. No longer playboy, newspaperman, or politician, he was now "Dr. Roosevelt." As new patients arrived, Franklin eagerly introduced them to the program of water exercise and swim therapy he had developed for himself. An orthopedic surgeon, Dr. Leroy Hubbard was hired to supervise treatment. By 1928, Warm Springs had sixty-one resident patients and was a widely-recognized center for hydro- or "water" therapy. For Franklin and the other patients the "magic" of the water seemed to work. Regular swimming strengthened muscles wasted by the disease. The massaging action of the spring gave life to damaged nerves. "There is now no question," Franklin wrote to a friend in 1926, "that this Warm Springs pool does my legs more good than anything else." He was convinced that in time he would be able to stand and perhaps even walk without the humiliating crutches.

He busied himself rebuilding the cottages and renovating the hotel. A new pool was constructed. With the help of Eleanor and his mother, Sara, he designed a cottage to live in. Although spartan in comparison to Springwood or the Roosevelt home in New York City, for Franklin this cottage was now home. He was going to stay in Warm Springs until he was cured.

One glorious autumn day in 1926, it looked as if it

might not take long. Franklin had been exercising in the pool. When he got out he decided, on impulse, to try and stand. Pulling himself up, he threw aside his crutches. For a few moments he stood alone, for the first time since his illness. The months of exercise had worked. The next challenge would be walking.

Franklin was becoming so involved in Warm Springs that people began to say he had forgotten about politics. He was no longer a contender, politicians told one another. He had bowed out of the race. Franklin did nothing to discourage this view. He enjoyed life at Warm Springs, he told everyone. He intended to stay there. The rolling hills of the Georgia countryside made a pleasant change from the smoke-filled conference rooms of his political life. He was getting stronger, too. A few more years and he would be up and walking. While he seemed to have no political plans, however, those who wrote Franklin out of politics were underestimating him. Franklin merely wanted to get well before he resumed his career. Franklin Delano Roosevelt was a fighter. His experiences had toughened him. He intended to reenter the political arena. He had hardly given up on politics, and during his time in Warm Springs two people made sure that politics did not give up on him.

The first was Louis Howe. The little man had big plans. One day, if Louis Howe had his way, Franklin would be president of the United States. Howe was determined to make sure the Democratic party did not forget Franklin. The industrious Howe wrote hundreds of letters to party leaders, members and organizers. He spoke to prominent politicians around the country. He made sure that when Franklin was ready to return, the party would be willing to help him. Howe kept Franklin's name alive in the Democratic party. But someone else kept the Roosevelt name alive in the minds of the American people, and that someone was Eleanor.

She had changed since her days as a shy "ugly duckling." She was now a political figure in her own right. No one was more active than Eleanor Roosevelt in fighting for causes near to the hearts of ordinary men and women. She was a strong supporter of women's rights, and of the rights of American workers. She fought hard for improvements in public schools and in the welfare system. She spoke her mind. Her honesty touched the voters who heard her. "Until Eleanor," one woman commented, "ordinary people felt left out of government. The leaders seemed as though they were somehow larger than life. But Eleanor is real, a wife and a mother, and the most accessible person in politics." She kept her husband in touch with the needs and desires of Americans in small towns, farm communities, and distant cities. These were places a crippled man could not go. Eleanor became his eyes and his ears. She traveled around the country, listening and learning. When she came home, she told Franklin what she had seen. She told him what upset people, what hurt them and what they needed. In her own way, Eleanor was becoming one of her husband's most valuable advisors. He learned a great deal from her.

Louis and Eleanor were keeping Franklin's political

hopes alive. Yet neither of them expected Franklin to re-enter politics in the near future. His health was their immediate concern.

In September, 1928 he got a phone call. It was his old friend, Al Smith. The Democratic Convention had just ended. Al was the Democratic nominee for president, and he needed Franklin's help. Smith had been governor of New York State for eight years. He was very popular there. The party needed someone to take his place. "It's crucial to my campaign," Al said. To help an old friend, would Franklin run for governor?"

Franklin hesitated. If he agreed, he would not have time to continue his therapy. He might never learn to walk again. "I OWE IT TO MY FAMILY AND MYSELF TO GIVE THE PRESENT CONSTANT IMPROVEMENT A CHANCE TO CONTINUE," he telegrammed Al. After much thought, Franklin decided not to run.

Louis agreed with him, but for political reasons. Smith didn't have a chance of winning. Under Republican leadership, the country was more prosperous than ever. "Don't do it, Franklin," Howe insisted. "Smith is going to lose, and if you run, you'll lose with him." Missy Lehand was also against it. She was sure that if Franklin ran for governor, he would never walk again. "Don't you dare!" she told him.

Franklin had begun to waver. Al was an old friend. Surely, he owed him a favor. Surely, he owed the Democratic party a favor. Al Smith sensed Franklin's uncertainty. He called his old friend again. "Would you refuse

Campaigning

to run if nominated at the New York State Convention?" he asked. Franklin did not answer. Smith, taking this as a "No," quietly hung up the phone.

The state convention was held on October 2, in Rochester. Eleanor was there. Franklin Delano Roosevelt was unanimously nominated. He was now the Democratic party's candidate for governor of New York.

Normally, this would have been an event for rejoicing, but the scene in Franklin's cottage in Warm Springs was far from cheerful. Missy Lehand sat in the corner in tears. "I just hope you don't win!" she told her boss. Howe had not even shown up, but Franklin and everyone else knew how upset he was. This was not part of his plan, and he was sure Franklin would lose. Franklin's other Warm Springs friends were equally upset. They knew this was the end of "Dr. Roosevelt" and his

Warm Springs Hydrotherapy Center. Suddenly a loud, cheerful voice, came bursting through the gloom: "Well, if I've got to run for governor, there's no use in all of us getting sick about it!" It was Franklin. The campaign was on!

CHAPTER FIFTEEN

A Candidate for President

O n November 7, 1928, Election Night, Al Smith and Franklin Delano Roosevelt waited together in the New York Armory. Election returns were flooding in. The hall was decorated for a party, but the two men were glum. Al Smith was losing the race for president. Herbert Hoover was winning reelection by a landslide. The Republican's slogan, "A chicken in every pot and a car in every garage," seemed to be just what the voters wanted. At last Al conceded the election. The tough, New York politician announced sadly that he was going to bed. Franklin did the same. His chances for governor were as good as Al Smith's chances to be president.

The next morning, Ed Flynn, head of the Bronx Democrats, woke Franklin up. "It's a miracle!" he told the astonished Franklin. *"You've won."*

On January 1, 1929 Franklin Delano Roosevelt was sworn in as governor in front of the Albany Statehouse. Beside Franklin on the podium stood Al Smith. The two men promised to work together as a team. Smith had always seen himself as Franklin's mentor—a more expe-

F.D.R. takes office of governor—ceremonial photo with Eleanor and mother

rienced politician helping along a "promising youngster."
He assumed that would continue now that Franklin was
governor, but things did not work out that way.

Al Smith had been governor of New York for eight
years. He knew the State of New York. He knew what

105

it needed. He hoped that Franklin would rely on him for help in his new job. He expected Franklin to ask his advice, take his suggestions. But during the first few months of his governorship, Franklin made it clear that he was his own man. Al Smith fumed in silence. What was Franklin doing? Finally his resentment burst out. "Do you know by God," he told a reporter, "that he has never consulted me about a damn thing since he has been governor? . . . He has *ignored* me!" It was the beginning of an open break between the two men. Franklin had not meant for it to come to this. But his fight with Al Smith signaled a major change in his political life. He was now a leader and he began to act like one.

He energetically attacked the problems confronting the state. Although he more or less followed the path laid out by Al Smith, Franklin was beginning to develop a political style of his own. He gathered together a team of his own advisors. Many of them were not the kind of people who had traditionally been in politics. Older state politicians wondered how such different men and women would be able to work together. As far as they were concerned, some of the people Franklin was giving jobs to were downright scandalous. Many of them were professors and social workers he met through Eleanor. They were a far cry from the old style, cigar-smoking, New York politician. Gasps were heard in genteel, drawing rooms across Albany when Franklin announced that MISS Frances Perkins would be his industrial commissioner— the person who would handle questions of business and labor. Could a *woman* handle a job like that? But Franklin insisted she was the person for the job. Soon everyone agreed with him. The serious-minded, thoughtful Miss Perkins soon proved she could handle New York State businessmen as well as any man.

Franklin had learned many lessons during his time in politics and now he was beginning to put them to use. If his advisors all seemed to have different backgrounds and ideas, it was because Franklin knew it was important to look at many sides of a question. He also knew how to get people to work together. The main feature of the Roosevelt style, however, was that he was willing to experiment; willing to try new and different ideas. This was to be vitally important. As 1929 drew to a close it became brutally clear that new ideas were just what New York State, and indeed all of America, badly needed.

The "roaring" twenties came crashing to a halt. The stock market had risen without stopping for several years. While this suggested that the economy was strong and healthy, there were warning signs that all was not well. The 1920s were "boom" years, and people were carried away by the optimism and high spirits of the post-war period. More and more, Americans invested in the stock market, hoping to make a quick profit. These new investors made stocks rise. Many of these people were buying stock on "margin"—this meant they bought the stocks on "credit" and paid for them later. People who had bought stock on margin watched with glee as the price of their stocks rose and rose. On paper, at least, these investors were making lots and lots of money. More and more of them began to live as though they already had it. Certain economists warned that the market was artificially high. The stocks did not reflect the real value of the companies they represented. Also, the stock market was riddled with corruption. It was not regulated by the government in any way. Many dishonest and unscrupulous investors took advantage of this. Men would form "stock pools"—trading stocks back and forth among themselves—to drive up the price. When the stocks hit an agreed-upon price, they would sell out, dumping the stocks on the market. The value would fall again. The smaller investors, the "suckers," would lose their money. Such dishonest practices made the market even more unstable.

In the fall of 1929 the market began to behave strangely. People grew worried. What happened next took everyone by surprise. On October 24, 1929, better remembered as "Black Thursday," the stock market suddenly crashed. All at once, millions of people rushed to trade in their stocks for money. The money simply was not there. So many people had bought stocks on margin, without actually ever paying for them, that the stocks had become virtually worthless. When people discovered that they could not get their money back, a panic started. In cities and small towns and farm communities across America, men and women flocked to their banks to withdraw their savings. The banks, however, had also placed their customers' money in stocks, bonds, and other investments. This is what banks normally do, keeping only part of their customers' money for use and withdrawal. But this time, the banks were in the same position as private investors. The stocks and securities that banks had invested in were suddenly worthless. The banks did not have enough money to pay back the hordes of customers now clamoring for their savings. Banks everywhere were forced to close—leaving their customers without a cent.

Overnight, millionaires and respectable middle-class people became paupers. The downward spiral continued. Factories and stores were forced to close. Millions of people lost their jobs. As the economy ground to a halt, these unemployed families could not find new jobs. The roaring twenties had ended. From the day of the crash, the United States had entered a period that would later be called the Great Depression. For people everywhere it was a time of misery and hardship.

Franklin saw the signs of the Depression all around him. In New York towns and cities, unemployed men filled the streets. Hungry families lined up at charity organizations for a cup of soup and a hunk of bread. Incredibly, the slide continued at an even faster rate. There was no end in sight to the suffering. The country waited for the Federal government to do something. Herbert Hoover, however, did not believe that government should interfere in the economy. Left alone, he believed, the American economy would soon return to prosperity. In the meantime things were getting rapidly worse. Prices fell so far that a steak dinner in a fine restaurant only cost about 35¢. Families were forced to leave their homes, and "Hoovervilles," shantytowns made of old cars, crates, and scraps, sprouted in vacant lots, parks, and fields across the country.

Franklin Delano Roosevelt felt something had to be done. In his campaign for reelection to a second term, he hammered this point home: it was time for the government to take a stand. The voters in New York responded with the largest victory of his career. The Great Depression was just the time for Franklin to put his ideas to work.

In March, Governor Roosevelt formed an emergency unemployment committee, and in August, established the Temporary Emergency Relief Administration (TERA). Headed by an energetic social worker named Harry Hopkins, it was the first agency of its kind in the country. Its purpose was to aid the jobless by providing food and shelter, and creating "work projects" which would put the jobless to work. Under TERA, workers built roads, planned parks, and refurbished public buildings. The idea caught on. Franklin's efforts did not go unnoticed. By the end of 1930, people were talking of him as a candidate for president in 1932.

As the Depression grew worse, Democratic hopes for the 1932 election soared. Americans wanted a change. Herbert Hoover's "sit back and wait" policy was plunging the country deeper and deeper into crisis. Voters were desperate, and the Republicans' philosophy of "hands off" government did little to help. The Democrats needed to provide voters with an alternative, and Franklin Delano Roosevelt seemed like the right man. In late 1930, Franklin declared his candidacy for the Democratic presidential nomination.

Louis Howe and Jim Farley, an experienced New York politician, headed his campaign. At the end of 1931, Al Smith declared his candidacy. Smith had not forgiven Franklin for ignoring him when he was governor. He was determined to prevent an easy Roosevelt victory. Smith planned to fight Franklin bitterly, and he had Tammany Hall behind him. The two former friends campaigned against one another through the long, dismal winter of 1931 and the spring that followed. When the Democratic Convention of 1932 came, both men were still in the race. The Democrats had no clear candidate.

Chicago was hot on June 27, 1932 and the convention floor was packed. Cigar-smoking delegates wheeled around the room, negotiating votes and heatedly debating the merits of their candidates. Franklin was at home in Hyde Park, but Jim Farley and Louis Howe were there to represent him. Howe's drinking and chain-smoking had caught up with him, and he was too sick to do the "legwork" of rounding up delegates' votes. So he sent Jim Farley to do it for both of them. Farley was an Irish Catholic, a deeply religious man who never touched a drink. Unlike Howe, who was famous for offending people, Farley was affable and charming.

Howe had rigged up a direct telephone line to Franklin at home in Hyde Park. He planned to give Franklin a blow-by-blow account of the convention. When the nominating process had ended and it was time to round up votes, Farley sprang into action. He spoke to John

"Nance" Garner, the burly leader of the Texas delegation. "Are you voting for Roosevelt?" Farley asked him. "If not, why not?" Farley argued persuasively. Garner finally agreed to support Franklin, under one condition: he wanted to be the candidate for vice-president. Farley conferred with Howe. Howe called Franklin. "We need Texas," Franklin said. "Besides, Garner is a good man." The deal was set. A Roosevelt victory began to seem more likely. Farley kept working. He spoke to men from Idaho, Michigan, Louisiana, and Nebraska. More delegates came over to the Roosevelt side. But Smith was still very much in the race. It looked as if the Democrats might once again have a deadlocked convention. Then the delegate from California, William McAdoo, mounted the speaker's podium. The hall went quiet. The convention was being broadcast by radio across the nation. In living rooms everywhere, people waited to hear what would happen. Back in Hyde Park, Franklin held his breath. Eleanor and the children sat beside him. McAdoo cleared his throat:

"California came here to nominate a president, she did not come to deadlock this convention. California casts all of its 44 votes for Franklin Delano Roosevelt!"

"Good old McAdoo!" Back in Hyde Park, Franklin, Eleanor, and the children burst into cheers. Farley and Howe slumped down in exhaustion. They had won.

Franklin Delano Roosevelt was the Democratic candidate for president.

That night, a plane took off from Albany to Chicago. Franklin was inside it along with Eleanor and members of his staff. He was flying out to accept the nomination in person. Traditionally, the candidate did not accept the nomination until several weeks later, but Franklin could not wait. It was a dramatic gesture for dramatic times. The plane flew across a country torn apart by poverty and hopelessness. People were waiting for some sign that things would change. Franklin wanted to make sure they got it.

There was wild applause when Franklin entered the convention hall in Chicago hours later. Using his crutches, he made his way to the podium. His speech appealed for a change of direction. The nation, he stated, was in a shambles. It was time for a new set of ideas to bring America out of its deep troubles. "I pledge you, I pledge myself to a new deal for the American people." Franklin called out in a voice hoarse with emotion, "Give me your help, not to win votes alone, but to win in this crusade to restore America to its people." The applause in the Chicago hall was deafening. Families across the United States listened to the speech on their radios, and believed Roosevelt could help them.

On Election Day, Franklin won 42 states—a sweeping victory. He went to bed knowing he would be president of the United States when he woke up. The country had almost never seen a darker time. The Depression was still in full swing. If anything, it was growing worse. And it was up to Franklin Delano Roosevelt to do something about it. He had won the campaign, and now he had to make his "New Deal" work.

CHAPTER SIXTEEN

A New Deal

M arch 4, 1933 was a cold, cloudy day in Washington, D.C. In the gray light, a crowd of thousands gathered in front of the Capitol Rotunda to witness the inauguration of Franklin Delano Roosevelt.

It was a desperate time. Almost all the banks in the country had closed their doors. You could not even cash a check in Washington, D.C. The nation's credit system had collapsed. Fear and uncertainty were everywhere. The Depression was at its worst and Americans were numb.

Silently, the crowd watched as Franklin Delano Roosevelt took the oath of office. Eleanor stood behind him, dressed in blue velvet. As the silence of the crowd intensified, Franklin turned to deliver his inaugural address. Across the country, millions of people sat beside their radios, or gathered in bars, grocery stores, and restaurants to hear him.

Franklin's voice rolled out high and strong across the crowd. To the millions listening, his speech was a call to battle. "*Let me assert my firm belief*," he began, "*that the only thing we have to fear is fear itself.*" In grim, measured tones he described the crisis facing the nation. The great-

F.D.R. at the Capitol

est task facing America, he said, was to put people back to work. Aid must be given to farmers, to those who had lost their homes. Steps must be taken to protect the nation's money supply. "The nation asks for action and action now," he stated.

The enormous crowd stirred slightly. The man before them seemed so hopeful, so confident. Perhaps there was a way to get the country on its feet after all. "It was very, very solemn and a little terrifying," Eleanor wrote later. "The crowds were so tremendous, and you felt they would do anything—if only someone would tell them what to do."

Rumors swirled through Washington. Franklin Roosevelt was bringing in a whole new team. Things would happen fast now. The entire country seemed to hold its breath, waiting. They did not have to wait long.

In the next three months, later known as the "Hundred Days," a record amount of legislation was passed. Almost all of it was aimed at easing the Depression. This group of laws, along with others passed afterwards, would become known as the "New Deal." These laws fundamentally changed the shape of the American government and the role it took in the lives of its citizens.

On that distant March day, however, Franklin only knew that he had to act quickly and firmly. He had no master plan, only a deep belief that new ideas had to be tried. He assembled his advisors, and the work began. President Roosevelt's cabinet contained a wider mixture of men and women than almost any before it. They ranged from his secretary of state, Cordell Hull, an old Tennessee mountain man, to Harold Ickes, the sharp-tongued, nature-lover and conservationist, who became his secretary of the interior. Franklin brought Miss Frances Perkins from New York to be his labor secretary. In addition to his official cabinet, Franklin also brought together a group of professors, lawyers, and other civilian experts. This informal group, nicknamed "the Brain

Trust," were behind many of the New Deal programs. One of the most important of these men was Harry Hopkins, the social worker Franklin had brought with him from Albany.

The White House was soon the scene of frenzied activity. Men in rumpled suits snatched a few hours sleep at their desks before getting back to the job. Reporters dashed to and fro. Press conferences were held in the president's office. Thick reports began to appear from the various offices around the building. A new mood was sweeping Washington. Things were happening.

On March 9, a mere week after his inauguration, Roosevelt announced the Emergency Banking Bill. The first act of Franklin's presidency, the bill was designed to restore the American banking system. It called for an immediate bank holiday. All the banks across the country were closed to give them a chance to reorganize. At breakneck speed, laws were passed to better regulate American banking. Meanwhile, each bank in the country was reviewed. Banks that still had money were reopened as quickly as possible. Others were taken out of business. It took time, but the banks that were left were reliable. People were beginning to feel they could trust the banks again. Those who had been hoarding money returned it to the banks. Badly needed money was circulated through the economy. The Emergency Banking Bill helped everybody from businessmen on Wall Street to farmers in Iowa. America's banking system was on solid ground again.

Franklin knew that his government had to help working Americans, those hardest hit by the Depression.

Millions of men and women were out of work. Many stood to lose their homes and their farms because they could not pay the mortgages. Thousands were literally starving. The situation called for drastic action.

On March 31, Franklin announced the formation of the Civilian Conservation Corps (CCC). This program used government money to put young men to work on projects for the "public good." Within months, around the country, young men were busy planting trees, building dams, clearing beaches, and restocking lakes and streams with fish. The CCC gave the embattled country hope. It was just the beginning.

Within weeks, Franklin and his advisors had devised a much more ambitious relief program. This was the Federal Emergency Relief Act (FERA). Five hundred million dollars was put aside to give direct help to states, cities, towns, and counties suffering under the Depression. Franklin wanted this money to get to people in need as directly as possible. The man he picked to set up the FERA programs did just that. Harry Hopkins was rapidly becoming one of Franklin's most trusted advisors.

Harry Hopkins was quite a character. His friends called him half do-gooder, half racetrack gambler. It was true that Hopkins loved betting, and spent much of his free time at the Laurel Track in nearby Maryland. He did not fit the picture of an important government official. He dressed in suits that could have come from the Salvation Army. But no one could work harder or faster than Harry Hopkins.

According to legend, the day FERA was signed into

law, Franklin said, *"Harry, get those people help fast."* Hopkins's desk had not even been moved into his office yet, so he sat in the hallway and within hours had sent out millions of dollars of relief, complete with instructions on how to spend it. He sent the money out so fast, *The New York Times* carried a worried headline the next morning reading: "MONEY FLIES!"

Under the energetic Hopkins, FERA sponsored another agency called the CWA, or Civil Works Administration. This program hired unemployed men and women to work on government projects. By January, 1934, over four million people had been employed. CWA workers built roads, schoolhouses, post offices, libraries, and airports—in short, any project Harry Hopkins could think of. Wealthy businessmen and industrialists criticized Harry Hopkins for spending money like water. Hopkins had one answer: "Hunger is not debatable." The program was putting hungry people to work. Men and women who had stood on street corners and begged for nickels and dimes were now getting paid for useful work.

Franklin Roosevelt agreed with him. So did most of the American people. The quick actions of President Roosevelt's government gave people a feeling that recovery was at hand. Americans were still poor, but they no longer felt alone. The CCC and the CWA were bringing Americans together to work for their country. The Works Progress Administration (WPA) was doing the same thing. Under the WPA, men and women were replanting forests and bringing electricity and water to the countryside. Writers, artists, actors, and musicians were

Depression "bread line"

hired to create art for the public. Plays and concerts were performed in town halls, libraries, and schools. WPA writers wrote guidebooks to the great cities, states, and regions of America. Photographers traveled around the country taking pictures of farmers and coal miners. Murals showing American life were painted on the walls of post offices. Many of these projects celebrated the American way of life, and gave people a new feeling of pride.

These work relief projects did much to lift the spirits

of people beaten down by poverty and unemployment. In May of 1933, acts were passed to protect people's farms and homes by refinancing their mortgages. This would keep more people from joining the ranks of the homeless. Roosevelt also signed into law an ambitious project called the National Industrial Recovery Act (NIRA).

The NIRA applied codes, or standards, to American businesses. These codes covered a wide range of issues, from pricing to setting fair hours and wages for workers. Some of the codes were designed to eliminate competition, others to protect workers, and still others to maintain quality in a wide variety of products. The NIRA tried to improve American business by making it more efficient and productive. It also gave the average American worker new rights. They could now negotiate with their bosses. Workers now had a voice in decisions which affected them. The symbol of the NIRA was a blue eagle. When stores and companies joined the NIRA, they put a big blue eagle sticker in their windows. As more and more blue eagles appeared in windows of grocery stores, restaurants and factories, it became a symbol of the new government. People looked at it proudly. The government was at last doing something for them.

Roosevelt's administration moved quickly to help farmers. The farmers had suffered all through the twenties, even when the rest of the country had been doing well. Overproduction had driven down the price of farm goods. The Agricultural Adjustment Act tried to do something about this. The government set levels of crop production—the amount of corn or cotton farmers in

America would grow. This, it was hoped, would stabilize prices at a high enough level for farmers to survive.

Soon Franklin's administration undertook even more radical efforts to help the poor in the countryside. The most famous of these was the TVA, the Tennessee Valley Authority Act. The Tennessee Valley had long been a poor area of the country. Soil was barren from overuse, and generations of farm communities had struggled to make ends meet. One man who felt this could be changed was George Norris, U.S. senator from Nebraska. He was a simple man who had thought deeply about the problems of the poor. He came to President Roosevelt with a plan. With planning, he said, the Tennessee Valley could be changed into a fertile, productive area. The great Tennessee River could provide great amounts of electricity if only dams were built. Harnessing this power would attract industry to the area, and the floods that hit the region every year could be controlled. With careful use of fertilizers, soil could be made fertile again. Norris argued that a program like this would improve the lives of people in the Tennessee Valley forever. They would no longer be a drain on the economy of the country, but self-sufficient citizens. Franklin agreed.

In May 1933, the great Tennessee Valley Project began. Dams were built to provide electric power. Experts worked to improve the soil and plan crops. The region grew more prosperous. Industries moved in. The TVA was the most ambitious example of regional planning ever undertaken in America and today it is looked upon as one of the most successful. As one historian

"Signs" of the New Deal

wrote: "It proved that a democratic government could by invention, farsighted planning and cooperation, benefit the entire society."

In 1935 the "New Deal" was completed with two acts. The first was the Wagner Act, named after the senator who had conceived it. The Wagner Act gave workers the right to organize into unions, and changed forever the relation between business and workers. The second was the Social Security Act of 1935. In this act, the federal government agreed to provide money for people who were unemployed or too old to work. These laws and benefits are taken for granted today, but in 1935, they were completely new—so new that many people felt a revolution had taken place. Americans began to speak more and more of the man responsible for the rapid changes: Franklin Delano Roosevelt.

"FDR," as he was called, was the most loved and hated man in America. He was loved by the ordinary men and women who had suffered through the Depression. They knew him mainly through his "fireside chats" on the radio. This practice, which Franklin had begun when he was governor of New York, became even more important now that he was president. Once a week he spoke directly to the American public, informally, as among friends. He explained to them what was going on in the country. He told them what his new programs were designed to do. He told them what it would take to get the economy working again. "We felt he cared about us," one woman said later of his "chats" on the radio. "He made us feel our country had been given back to us." Franklin made people feel that the government cared about them. For men and women who had lost their jobs, who had gone hungry, who had scraped and saved just to put food on the table for their children, and who had felt for so long that no one cared, this in itself, was enough to make them fiercely loyal to FDR.

Franklin's critics, however, called him a "demagogue." They said he fooled the ordinary American people by making them believe he was on their side, while the New Deal laws were destroying the fabric of American life. Now that the government was taking care of them, Americans would become lazy. They would lose their do-it-yourself spirit. Many of these critics were businessmen, who had always operated pretty much as they pleased. With the New Deal, the government was involved in commerce, and not necessarily on their side. Businessmen could now be told what was a fair wage and how to treat their employees. They resented it.

Franklin's harshest critics, however, were families with "old wealth"—the people he had grown up with. They felt he was a "traitor to his class." How could one of their own raise taxes, place restrictions on business, and start a system of welfare? Such people called Franklin a "dangerous radical." Franklin was hurt by this. It was like being rejected by the Porcellain Club all over again. He did not see himself as a radical. He was a politician. Franklin once told Eleanor: "Politics is not ideas, it is people." He meant that a democratic government had to respond to its people. It had to give them what they needed and wanted at the time. A good politician, as far as Franklin was concerned, understood that. So, while many were angered and puzzled by the New Deal—especially coming from a son of the wealthy—Franklin saw it as the will of the people. In 1936 election was approaching, and he planned to run again.

There was one dark spot on the horizon. Louis Howe, Franklin's oldest and most trusted political mentor, was near death. The little man had been cut down by a lifetime of smoking hard, drinking hard, and working harder than anyone. He lay in an oxygen tent in Bethesda Naval Hospital. Eleanor visited him often and beside his bed was a phone—a direct line to the president. The two old friends would stay up late talking. Franklin encouraged Louis to get better. But the little man knew what was coming. "I'm done for," he said to his boss. "You'll do fine without me."

On April 15, 1935, the flags all along the White House flew at half-mast. The "man who made the president" was gone. The crusty political mastermind had remained fiercely loyal to Franklin to the end. "I've been as close to Franklin Roosevelt as a valet," he told a reporter a few months before his death, "and he is still a hero to me."

The little man would have been happy with the election results of November 7, 1936. The American people had voted in a landslide for Franklin Roosevelt. The New Dealers were in for a second term.

CHAPTER SEVENTEEN

The Great Storm

R arely had any president been in a better position than Franklin Delano Roosevelt at the start of his second term. The reforms of his New Deal were working to pull America out of its economic illness. The voters were behind him. People everywhere felt they knew "FDR" personally. He was their friend, the man who had stood up for them against the "rich bosses." He had given hope during the terrible bleak days of the Depression. Eleanor, too, was a beloved First Lady. In her shabby suits and funny hats, (which one reporter described as looking as if they had recently been dragged out from under the bed) she was a familiar figure as she traveled about the country, investigating the conditions of farm workers in Iowa, or visiting coal miners in Kentucky. People saw Franklin and Eleanor not as distant politicians, but as real people who cared about them. Although the country was still in trouble, a new spirit was in the air, and Franklin was responsible for it. The country believed, as Franklin told them: "Our future belongs to us Americans. It is for us to design it; for us to build it."

As 1937 passed into 1938, however, the New Deal no longer seemed so "new." Many began to take the

Eleanor as First Lady—visible public figure

changes for granted, and to criticize Franklin for what it had failed to accomplish. Unemployment had not disappeared. The country was far from prosperous. Businessmen said the New Deal had created conflict between rich and poor in America. The president was blamed. Franklin had other, perhaps more serious, problems to worry about as well. Europe seemed to be rushing headlong into another great war, not twenty years after the "War to End All Wars." Franklin did not see how America could stay out of it. Yet that was just what America wanted to do.

By 1938, Italy had taken over Ethiopia. Germany had taken over Austria and Czechoslovakia. Meanwhile in the Far East, Japan had invaded part of China. Germany, Italy, and Japan were determined to invade and conquer other countries, to build empires. While America could afford to look the other way from its safe perch across the Atlantic, France and England could not. Their countries might get taken over as well.

The country that France and England feared most was Germany. Since 1933, Germany's leader was a powerful man with strange, troubling ideas. The man's name was Adolf Hitler. When Americans first saw newsreels of Hitler, many wanted to laugh. He was a funny looking, short man with a big moustache. When he spoke he used exaggerated gestures, and his voice was high and squeaky. What he said, however, was not so funny, and worse, many Germans seemed to hang on to his every word. Their country was in trouble. Hitler appealed to them by blaming everyone else for their troubles, and preaching a policy based on hatred and prejudice.

Germany's troubles had begun at the end of the first World War. Germany's government had fallen apart. The war had reduced Germany's cities and towns to charred ruins. Its industries had shut down. The Treaty of Versailles demanded that Germany pay back France and England for the damage done to their countries. To trim Germany's power further, all Germany's colonies were taken away and sections of her land were removed to help form the new countries of Czechoslovakia and Yugoslavia. The Germans, always a proud and strong people, now felt disgraced, poor, and weak. They wanted to regain their prominence. The German economy, like that of America, grew worse and worse during the late 1920's. By 1930, the German currency, the mark, was worthless. Germans grew angry and desperate. They needed someone to inspire them, and they found that person in Adolf Hitler.

Hitler was a mesmerizing speaker. He inflamed German crowds by speaking in hysterical terms of Germany's enemies. He said these enemies were holding Germany back from the glorious future she deserved. France, England, and the United States were to blame for Germany's poverty. Germany was too small. It needed more room to become strong and powerful again. It was Germany's destiny, Hitler said, to take over the world, and establish a German empire that would stretch over all the continents of the world. Lastly, Hitler blamed the Jews for Germany's problems. He said they were the foundation of the conspiracy against the German people. He began to speak of punishing the Jews, of pushing them out of German society, of making them outcasts. He said the Jews were the evil influence that had led Germany into financial and social ruin. In time, this was to lead to the most horrifying part of Germany under Hitler: The Final Solution. The Final Solution was a secret plan to systematically exterminate, or murder, all the Jews of Europe. This is called genocide. As Hitler's power grew, "work" or "labor" camps were established in isolated parts of the German and Polish countryside. Here, six million Jews would eventually die in Hitler's notorious gas chambers in scenes too horrific to seem quite real to the shocked world who learned about them only when the war had ended. In 1936, however, this was still in the future. There were merely disturbing reports of Hitler's gospel of hatred, and his warlike speeches to the German people. Hitler called himself and his political party National Socialists, or Nazis for short. Once he came into power, he assumed more and more control over every part of German life. He demanded absolute obedience from every German, whether or not they agreed with him. German people could no longer do as they wished; they could not even voice their opinions anymore. With the German people under his control, Hitler turned his sights outward. By 1939, he had taken over Austria and Czechoslovakia, and now he wanted Poland.

France and England told Hitler that if he attacked Poland, they would declare war against him. By then, Hitler had made a deal with Italy. If Germany went to war, Italy would join on Germany's side. In September 1939, German troops stormed through Poland. France and England declared war.

The second World War had begun.

Thousands of miles away, Japan was developing a similar plan of world domination. The slogan *Hakko Ichiu*, or "bringing the eight corners of the world under one roof," was the rallying cry of the war-hungry, General Tojo. The Japanese pushed to take over China—as the first part of their plan to establish an empire they called the "Greater East Asia Co-Prosperity Sphere." They

War begins in Europe

drove the Americans and English out of China. At first these efforts were subtle, but they soon became more warlike. In December 1937, they bombed and sunk the SS *Panay*, a U.S. gunboat, as it traveled down the Yangtze River. Americans protested. Many worried it would lead to direct confrontation. Then Japan apologized. Americans breathed a sigh of relief. They did not want to go to war.

Franklin Roosevelt felt that eventually America would have no choice. The Japanese warlords and Hitler were determined to dominate the world. It was only a matter of time before they directly threatened American safety. At the end of 1937, Roosevelt called out for a "quarantine of aggressor nations." The American public reacted angrily. Newspapers, magazines, and private citizens told Franklin in no uncertain terms to "stay out of foreign affairs." Americans had bitter memories of the first World War. They had not forgotten the wasteful deaths of thousands upon thousands of men—their fathers, brothers, and sons. Americans had rarely been more firmly in favor of peace. Students held meetings and gave speeches in support of "neutrality," or keeping out of the fight. Businessmen argued in favor of "isolationism," or that America should stay out of the affairs of the rest of the world, and in the U.S. Congress, Senator Gerald Nye of South Dakota staged hearings to prove that the coming war was the work of arms merchants or merchants of death who encouraged war for profit alone. The nation felt so strongly about staying out of Europe's war that between 1935 and 1939 laws were passed forbidding private loans or the sale of weapons to any country at war. Franklin had not forgotten the sights he had seen on the battlefields of World War I. But he could not help being sympathetic to England and France in their fight against Hitler. And the situation in Europe was rapidly growing worse.

In April 1940 the Germans, acting with lightning speed, overran Denmark and Norway. They did not intend to stop there. On May 10, the German army invaded neutral Belgium; then they marched into Holland. Europe was falling like a stack of dominoes before the mighty Nazi army.

By June the Germans had made deep inroads into France. On June 15, Paris was taken over. Soon half of France was German-occupied. In all of Europe, only England remained free. President Roosevelt knew that if England fell it was only a matter of time before Hitler turned his sights on America. The Americans had to help England *now!*

Roosevelt was in close contact with England's prime minister, Winston Churchill. An iron-willed man with a face like a bulldog, Churchill's courage inspired the English in their dark hour. His speeches lifted the wavering spirits of the country. Churchill was determined that his country would never fall before the Nazis. He told the British people:

"We shall not flag or fail; we shall go on to the end; we shall fight in France; we shall fight on the seas and oceans; we shall fight on the landing grounds; we shall fight in the fields and in the streets. . ."

But Churchill desperately needed the Americans. Germany was a larger country than England, with a formidable army and air force. Churchill knew that Hitler was planning an invasion by sea at any moment. England's chances for victory looked slim. Churchill begged Roosevelt for fifty destroyers to defend the English coastline. Roosevelt was willing, but his hands were tied. He could not send the destroyers to England without putting a bill before Congress. This might take months, and England needed the destroyers immediately. Churchill pushed Roosevelt—"Mr. President," he cabled, "in the long history of the world this is a thing to do *now!*" At the final hour, Franklin devised a solution. America would lend destroyers to England in exchange for being given leases to England's air and naval bases in the Caribbean, Newfoundland, and Bermuda. The destroyers were sent and no laws were broken.

The president had taken a big political risk. By sending ships to England, he was bending American neutrality. Newspapers began calling him a "warmonger."

In 1940, Franklin ran for a third term. This was the first time in American history a president had run a third time. His opponent, Wendell Willkie, a self-made Indiana businessman, made war the big issue of the campaign. A third term for Roosevelt, he argued, would bring with it war. "Our boys are already almost on the transports," he shouted in speech after speech. Roosevelt's advisors grew alarmed. Americans did not want a war. Franklin's standing dropped daily in the opinion polls. *Time* magazine and *The New York Times* came out for Willkie. Aside from the war issue, people worried that it was dangerous to have one man serve as president for too long.

Franklin did not see how America could stay out of the European conflict. In September, he called for the passage of the Selective Service Act, the compulsory drafting and military training of American men when they turned twenty-one. It was a bold step. Franklin felt certain it was necessary.

He toured the country giving speeches, hoping to persuade the voters that they could not remain detached from the rest of the world. He stopped short of saying America should go to war. Opposition to war was just too strong. Nevertheless he tried to convince Americans that they had to take a stand. He told them:

> There is a great storm raging now, a storm that makes things harder for the world. And that storm, which did not start in this land of ours, is the true reason I would like to stick by this people of ours—stick by until we reach the clear, sure footing ahead. We will make it and the world, we hope, will make it too.

On Election Day, 1940, the American people elected Franklin Delano Roosevelt, president. Now he had to decide what to do about the situation in Europe—and in Japan.

Franklin moved quickly. In January 1941, he passed

the Lend-Lease Act. This allowed the president to sell, exchange, lease or lend American weapons to any country whose defense the president felt was essential to the United States. Until then, the Allies had only been able to buy weapons by paying cash for them. This was hard for England, as their funds were low. Now, Franklin could send weapons to the British whether they could pay or not.

Americans saw that they were becoming more involved in the Allied cause. Public opinion was slowly changing. As people saw pictures of London being bombed, and heard Winston Churchill's stirring speeches on the radio or saw newsreels of the mighty German Army on the march, they began to realize that there was no choice. The Nazis were a menace to the entire world.

In May, President Roosevelt declared an "unlimited national emergency." German submarine U-boats were sinking American ships in the Atlantic. In August, Franklin met with Winston Churchill off the coast of Newfoundland. The two men drew up an agreement, called the Atlantic Charter, stating the principles which the United States and England shared. It proclaimed freedoms which all nations had a right to, and promised to defend these freedoms.

In July, Japan declared it was in command over all of French Indochina. President Roosevelt responded sternly by cutting off exports of rubber, iron, and oil to Japan—a severe blow to the Japanese warlords. They needed American oil to keep their war machine operating.

Pearl Harbor

America said it would give Japan oil if they would move out of China and Indochina. Japan refused. The two countries were at a stalemate. The Americans did not know it, but the Japanese had already moved to break the stalemate. They wanted war with America. On December 2, a coded telegram was sent to a convoy of Japanese carriers stationed in the Kurile Islands in the Pacific. It read *"Climb Mount Nitkaya,"* Japanese code for "Attack!"

Five days later, the Japanese carriers reached their firing point 275 miles north of Pearl Harbor, the large American naval base on Hawaii. At 7:55 A.M., bombs began to fall on the quiet harbor. Two minutes later, Admiral Bellinger, naval air commander of Pearl Harbor sent a broadcast over the wires:

AIR RAID PEARL HARBOR—THIS IS NO DRILL

Franklin was informed shortly afterwards. Japan's sneak attack on Pearl Harbor had left 2,403 Americans dead and 1,178 wounded. The finest battleships of the U.S. Navy's Pacific Fleet lay at the bottom of the harbor. America was in the war.

CHAPTER EIGHTEEN

"A Strong, Active Faith"

O n December 8, 1941, the United States officially entered World War II. It was up to Franklin Delano Roosevelt to lead the country through the difficult fight ahead.

He had been president for nine years, and the pressures of the office had taken their toll on him. His face was more wrinkled. When he was tired his hands trembled. But his famous smile had not changed, nor had his boundless optimism. His speeches once again inspired American families, as they had in the darkest months of the Depression. "No matter how long it may take us," Roosevelt's voice was heard to say on radios around the country, "the American people in their righteous might will win through to absolute victory."

It was a strange Christmas. All men between eighteen and forty-four were expected to enter the armed services. As Christmas trees went up, men in all corners of the country were shipping out to distant ports and army bases around the world. Blackout curtains were put up in the White House. Factories roared into action, providing the weapons and supplies America and its allies would need to win the war. Women by the thousands were going to work, taking the place of the men who were going to war. Even the president's family was affected. A friend who phoned Eleanor late in December found her in tears. She and the president had said goodbye to their sons that same morning. "If only by the law of averages," Eleanor said quietly, "they may never come back." The same scene was taking place in households across America. Through it all, President Roosevelt remained firm, calm, and hopeful.

On December 22, Winston Churchill arrived in Washington. The two Allied leaders were to decide on their war strategy. The White House was transformed into a "command post." Maps were pinned to the walls and strategies were discussed deep into the night by solemn generals. On New Year's Day 1942, the Allied countries (including England, the Soviet Union, and China, among others) issued a joint declaration. In it they stated their aims in fighting the war and their determination to defeat Hitler's Germany and their Japanese allies.

Roosevelt gathered his staff. Harry Hopkins was now his most trusted advisor, and did much of the negotiating with Churchill and the other Allies. Roosevelt's chief of staff was General George C. Marshall of Virginia. There was no better man for the job. A patient, wise, military leader, Marshall was a man people said "looked as though he should have been carved out of granite." He inspired his troops and commanded with a keen sense of strategy. The head of the air force was the amiable, efficient General H. H. "Hap" Arnold, and the navy was commanded by the steely-eyed Admiral Ernest King, who, as one observer put it, "seldom if ever made a mistake." Under these men, the American armed forces would eventually prove a formidable threat. But at first, all the news was bad. Wake Island, Guam, and the Philippines fell to the Japanese. Americans were stunned. They had never before been defeated by a foreign power like this.

On February 23, 1942, Franklin held a special fireside chat to talk about the war. As Americans gathered anxiously around their radios, Franklin asked them to have a map of the world open in front of them. He then explained in simple, concrete terms what the American forces hoped to achieve. Tracing the elaborate path of the war throughout the world, he told them what was happening, and where the greatest difficulties lay. "If the people understand the problem and what we are driving at," he told a speech writer, "I am sure they can take any kind of bad news right on the chin." Roosevelt's speech reassured his listeners. The world was under siege, the fight was just beginning, and together Americans would pull through it.

Average citizens banded together to help the war effort. War bonds were sold at rallies to raise money for weapons and supplies. Schoolchildren collected soda cans, so the tin could be used to manufacture needed weapons. Housewives and young girls knit socks and stitched shirts to send to servicemen abroad. People even turned in old Gramophone records to be melted down

143

and used for making weapons. Others planted "victory gardens," growing their own fruit and vegetables to protect against the food shortages. War songs and jingles sprang up. Hollywood films celebrated the men and women fighting on the front lines. The country was gearing up for the fight.

The first hopeful news came over the airwaves in August. Russians had stopped the German forces in Stalingrad. Losses on both sides had been horrific. The battle gave the Allies heart. Once again, Hitler had been stopped just short of achieving total command over Europe. The Allies prepared to strike back. Plans were laid in Washington state rooms. The first plan, a secret outside the Allied chambers of command, was given the code name "Operation Torch."

Under the command of U.S. General Dwight Eisenhower and the British General Sir Bernard Montgomery, "Operation Torch" was put into action in October. The Allies were to invade North Africa, then completely overrun by the Nazis. If the Allies managed to free North Africa, they would have a foothold through which they could enter Europe (by way of Italy). The plan was risky, but it worked. By May of 1943, the British and American armies had defeated the Germans in North Africa. The tide of the war was turning. The Allies were in position to make their strike on Europe.

Throughout the winter of 1943, the Allied army set its sights on liberating Italy. Mounting attacks on the German forces there, they slowly advanced into Italian territory. The fighting was brutal. As one war correspon-

dent wrote, the American G.I.s often had to live "like
men of prehistoric times." The countryside was cold. Allied soldiers marched through mile after mile of frost and
mud across some of the most mountainous country in
Europe. At last, on June 4, 1944, the Allies liberated
Rome. But two days later even more exciting news came
over the newswires to the British and American civilians
waiting anxiously at home: the Allied armies had landed
on the French coast in the province of Normandy.

The invasion of Normandy, code-named "D-Day,"
was the turning point of World War II. Plans for the
invasion began early in 1943, when Roosevelt, Churchill
and their chiefs of staff decided that the Normandy coast
must be their target. General Dwight Eisenhower had
been appointed commander of the invasion. The mild-
mannered, practical commander had surveyed the de-
tailed planning. Ships and planes would approach the
Normandy coast in bursts, attacking the Germans with
wave upon wave of troops and artillery.

Everything was in place the morning of June 4. The
skies above the English Channel were cloudy and the
wind was high. The airmen were worried. Wasn't the
weather too rough? General Eisenhower hesitated. The
weather was not ideal, but a delay might be even more
dangerous. Hitler expected an Allied attack. A formidable
German defense of radar and guns had been built up all
along the Normandy shore. Hitler did not know when
the invasion would take place, however. Eisenhower was
almost sure if they went now, they would take the Germans by surprise. "I don't like it," Eisenhower said, look-

ing at the sky, "but we'll go." With these words, the largest invasion by water ever to take place began. In orderly streams, warships, carriers, planes, and destroyers streamed out from the English coast. The Allies would attempt to land on the beaches of Normandy the next morning.

Two thousand miles across the Atlantic in Charlottesville, Virginia, a man in a wheelchair looked out the window of a wooden frame house with a worried expression on his face. Franklin Delano Roosevelt had been involved in every phase of planning the invasion. The crucial moment was fast approaching. The president was supposed to be spending the weekend relaxing with friends. Even those who did not know what was going on, however, noticed how tense the president seemed. His hands trembled. At times he seemed to be praying. As darkness fell on Charlottesville, phone wires lit up. All through the night calls went back and forth between the Pentagon, the White House, and the president. Were the Allies getting through? It was not until morning that confirmed reports began to come in. The invasion of Normandy was a success. The fighting had been hard and bitter. Many men had been lost, but the Allies were now safely in Europe.

That night, Franklin led the nation in prayer. In homes everywhere, people prayed with him. "Lead our sons, pride of our nations, straight and true, give strength to their arms, stoutness to their hearts, steadfastness in their faith." The nation was on edge. The worst fighting passed. Victory was no longer in doubt.

In the Pacific also, the American forces were gaining. In 1942, American troops defeated Japan in a ferocious battle for the South Pacific island of Guadalcanal. The Americans established a base there. Throughout 1943, the U.S. Navy gained control of the waters around Japan. In June of 1944, the two opposing countries met head-to-head one hundred miles northwest of Guam. The Battle of the Philippine Sea, as it was called, wiped out Japan's air force and severely damaged its navy. Japan did not recover. By August, 1944, the Americans had reclaimed Guam. Japan did not have the industrial strength to build up again, while the American war machine showed no signs of flagging. Even so, the real end of the war would not come for some time.

Factories remained open day and night. People followed the progress of the Allied armies through newspapers and radios. They comforted each other when casualties were bad. They cheered when the Allies won major victories. The news came that the Allies had reclaimed France. Allied soldiers were beginning the long march to Berlin.

Another election was approaching. Americans felt only one man could lead them through this difficult time: Franklin Delano Roosevelt. Franklin accepted the Democratic nomination, but he refused to campaign. "In these days of tragic sorrow," he explained, "I do not consider it fitting." He won anyway. He chose a new vice-president, a plain-spoken Missourian named Harry S. Truman.

Three days after his fourth inauguration he set off

on the cruiser *Quincy* for the city of Yalta in the Crimea. There, Roosevelt would meet with Winston Churchill and Joseph Stalin. Although the war in the Pacific was still raging, the Allied forces were marching across the Rhine. Hitler's kingdom was crumbling. Roosevelt, Churchill, and Stalin, the "Big Three," had called a conference to discuss what should be done when the fighting ended. Europe was reeling after six years of all-out war. Cities on both sides were bombed shells. The astonished world was learning more about Hitler's death camps, places such as Belsen, Dachau, and Auschwitz whose names would later be known the world over as symbols of man's inhumanity to man. The three leaders had to decide what the shape of Europe should be when the fighting had ended.

Roosevelt was a tired man. Many of his old friends had died. His mother, Sara, had passed away in September of 1940. She had been such a great influence on him since his childhood, and he could not believe the Hyde Park house was empty of her strong presence. "Perhaps," he told Eleanor sadly, "she went at the right time. I don't think she would like the post-war world." It was one of the few times Eleanor saw him cry openly. In July 1944, his loyal secretary Missy Lehand died of a stroke. His loneliness increased. Eleanor was almost always away from home, working for various causes. His four sons were away in the army. Worse, his dear friend and confidant, Harry Hopkins, was mortally ill with cancer. As Franklin contemplated the great task of rebuilding, he felt old.

"Big Three" conference

Yalta was hot and humid. The negotiations between the three men were difficult. It was clear to Roosevelt and Churchill that Stalin, the leader of the Communist Soviet Union, had ideas of his own. He was already planning to take over Eastern Europe and make those nations Soviet colonies. Roosevelt and Churchill sensed that Stalin could not be trusted. While they mistrusted the Soviet leader, they needed him. The war was not yet over, and the Soviet Union was their ally. Both Roosevelt and Churchill felt they had no choice but to treat Stalin as a partner.

To the other negotiators, Franklin often appeared like a "sick old man." Although there were flashes of his old wit and good humor, his eyes often strayed. At times his expression became blank. His personal doctor had known for a long time that the president's heart was weakening, but now it was rapidly growing worse.

Two days after he returned from Yalta, President Roosevelt addressed the Congress on the conference. As he came into the room, the assembled senators, congressmen and reporters drew in their breath. He was sitting down in a wheelchair. Although Franklin had never learned to walk once he had left Warm Springs, somehow no one had ever thought of him as a cripple. He had always stood strong and tall when he gave speeches, as if he used neither crutches nor braces. Now, however, he looked like an invalid. Everyone there took in his gray complexion, his tired eyes, and his trembling hands. Franklin's speech was long and rambling. Few paid attention to it. They were all looking at the man who had led them for so long and through such difficult times. When the speech was over, the crowd rose to its feet and gave F.D.R. a standing ovation. He was too tired to acknowledge it. He slid down further in his wheelchair and was led out by his aides. Everyone in the silent room wondered if they would ever see Franklin Delano Roosevelt alive again.

Two months later on April 12, 1945, in Warm Springs, Georgia, the man who had served as president longer than any man before or after, died of a massive brain hemorrhage at three o'clock in the afternoon. He had been writing a speech for Thomas Jefferson Day. The

Flag-draped coffin

last words he wrote, just hours before his death, were characteristic: "The only limit to our realization of tomorrow will be our doubts of today. Let us move forward with strong, active faith." The president was gone. As news of his death spread, all across America flags were flown at half-mast. People reacted with fear, disbelief, and grief. A procession of funeral cars, led by Eleanor Roosevelt and her husband's flag-draped coffin, made its slow way from Warm Springs to the railway station and then to Washington. There the official processional was led by Eleanor and Harry S. Truman, the new president of the United States. On Saturday, April 14, Franklin's coffin was put on a train going to New York City.

It was a cool, bright spring day in Hyde Park. A brisk breeze stirred across the rose garden of Springwood, where Franklin had played so often as a boy. The assembled crowd did not seem to notice the new leaves, or the flowers that bloomed all around. Their heads were bent and their eyes were downcast. As a military band played, the flag-draped coffin was laid in its final resting place. Franklin Delano Roosevelt, who had traveled so far and seen so many changes, was home at last.

Albany
Capital of New York State.

Blackballing
Ceremony by which prospective members of fraternities or social clubs in universities were accepted or rejected.

Black Thursday
October 24, 1929. The day the stock market crashed, signaling the beginning of the Depression.

Boss System
System whereby certain politicians called "Bosses" controlled the political life of towns, cities, and states through political organizations known as "machines." Bosses were usually corrupt and were associated with bribery and other crimes.

Campobello
Roosevelt's summer home, an island off the coast of New Brunswick, Canada.

Churchill, Winston
Prime Minister of England during World War II.

Civilian Conservation Corps (CCC)
Agency formed during the New Deal to put young men left unemployed by the Depression to work on projects for the public good.

Coming Out

Period in which wealthy young girls make their formal entrance into society.

Crimson

Harvard University's daily newspaper. Franklin Delano Roosevelt worked on the paper during his time at college.

Daniels, Josephus

Secretary of the navy under Woodrow Wilson. Franklin Delano Roosevelt's boss as assistant secretary of the navy.

D-Day

June 6, 1944. The day the Allies carried out the invasion of Normandy which began the recapture of Europe from Nazi Germany.

Delano, Fred

Franklin Delano Roosevelt's uncle.

Delano, Warren

Franklin Delano Roosevelt's grandfather.

Derby

Type of hat worn by men in Franklin Delano Roosevelt's time.

Duchess County

County of New York State where Roosevelt's hometown of Hyde Park was located. Franklin Delano Roosevelt represented Duchess County as state senator.

Eisenhower, General Dwight

General of American army during World War II. 34th president of the United States.

Farley, James
Franklin Delano Roosevelt's campaign manager in 1932 election.

Fireside Chats
Franklin Delano Roosevelt's radio talks to the American public. One of the most popular features of his presidency.

Fourteen Points
President Woodrow Wilson's fourteen-point plan for lasting peace between nations after World War I.

Great Depression
Time of economic crisis and personal hardship in America lasting from 1932 until World War II.

Groton Academy
Prep school in Connecticut that Franklin Delano Roosevelt attended.

Grotonian
Groton's school newspaper.

Harding, Warren G.
29th president of the United States.

Harvard
Oldest university in the United States (located in Cambridge, Massachusetts). Franklin Delano Roosevelt's college.

Hirohito, Emperor
Japan's Emperor during World War II.

Hitler, Adolf
Leader of Germany from 1933 to 1945. Head of the Nazi party, he was a dictator who led Germany into World War II.

Hoover, Herbert
31st president of the United States. Defeated by Franklin Delano Roosevelt in 1932.

Hopkins, Harry
Social worker who became Franklin Delano Roosevelt's most trusted and valuable advisor during the New Deal and World War II.

Howe, Louis
Franklin Delano Roosevelt's political mentor and campaign manager. He was called "The man who made the president."

The Hundred Days
First hundred days of Franklin Delano Roosevelt's presidency. The period when most of the "New Deal" legislation was passed, and a record number of bills voted on and passed by Congress.

Hyde Park
Franklin Delano Roosevelt's birthplace.

Insurgents
Group of "rebel" New York State assemblymen involved in Franklin Delano Roosevelt's 1911–12 fight with Tammany Hall. Roosevelt was chairman of the group.

Invasion of Normandy
Allied invasion of the French coast in June, 1944.

League of Nations
President Wilson's plan for a league or group of nations who would settle their disputes through negotiation and compromise rather than war.

Lehand, Missy
Franklin Delano Roosevelt's secretary.

Lusitania
Ship sunk by German submarines on May 7, 1915, helped bring Americans into World War I.

Mark
German currency.

Marshall, General George C.
Chief of American Armed Forces during World War II.

McKinley, William
25th president of the United States. Assassinated in September, 1901.

Muckrakers
Journalists who reported misbehavior or scandalous actions of prominent people.

Murphy, "Boss" Charles F.
Boss Tweed's successor, and head of Tammany Hall during Franklin Delano Roosevelt's time.

National Industrial Recovery Act (NIRA)
New Deal act, passed June 16, 1933, designed to better organize and regulate American business.

Nazis
Adolf Hitler's party, The National Socialists.

Neutral
Term for country that does not take sides in a war.

New Deal
Franklin Delano Roosevelt's policies during the Depression.

Pearl Harbor
December 7, 1941. The Japanese attack on American naval base at Pearl Harbor in Hawaii brought America into World War II.

Perkins, Frances

Franklin Delano Roosevelt's labor secretary. The first woman to occupy the position.

Porcellian

Harvard's most exclusive social club from which Franklin Delano Roosevelt was rejected as a student.

Progressive Era

America under Woodrow Wilson (early 1900s), a time of interest in social reform.

Roosevelt, Eleanor

Franklin Delano Roosevelt's wife. A strong political force in her own right, Eleanor fought for a variety of humanistic causes, including women's rights.

Roosevelt, Franklin Delano

32nd president of the United States. Architect of the "New Deal."

Roosevelt, James

Franklin Delano Roosevelt's father.

Roosevelt, Sara Delano

Franklin Delano Roosevelt's mother.

Roosevelt, Theodore

Franklin Delano Roosevelt's fifth cousin. 26th president of the United States.

Rough Riders

Regiment Teddy Roosevelt led during Spanish American War.

Spanish-American War

War between United States and Spain over rights of Cuba in 1898.

Springwood

Franklin Delano Roosevelt's family estate in Hyde Park.

Square Deal

Theodore Roosevelt's plan to carry out social reforms during his presidency. Name given his domestic policies.

Stalin, Joseph

Leader of Communist Soviet Union during World War II. America's ally during the war.

State Senator

Representative to state legislature. First elected position Franklin Delano Roosevelt held.

Tammany Hall

Name of New York State political "machine."

Tennessee Valley Authority Act (TVA)

New Deal program to improve conditions in the Tennessee Valley by using government funds to develop resources (energy, soil, and so on) of the region.

Tojo, General Hideki

Japanese leader during World War II.

Tweed, "Boss" William

Legendary Tammany Hall boss.

Wagner Act

July 5, 1935. Set guides for labor relations in America and gave workers the right to organize and join trade unions.

Wilson, Woodrow

28th president of the United States.

Yalta Conference

Meeting between Franklin Delano Roosevelt, Winston Churchill, and Joseph Stalin at the end of World War II to discuss what would be done when the war ended. February, 1945.

1. What major event finally got the United States involved in World War II?
2. What were President Franklin Delano Roosevelt's "Fireside Chats?" What was the purpose of them? Do you think they were a good idea?
3. Name and describe three government agencies Franklin Delano Roosevelt established during the New Deal.
4. From your reading of the book, compare the 1920s with the 1930s in the United States.
5. Who was Louis Howe? Why was he called "the man who made the president?"
6. Was Eleanor Roosevelt a typical First Lady? How was she different? How did she help her husband?
7. Name three reasons why the United States entered World War II.
8. What was the Great Depression?
9. Research Tammany Hall. Explain what the "boss system" was.
10. In his first speech as president in 1932, Franklin Delano Roosevelt said, "The only thing we have to fear is fear itself." What did he mean by this? Do you think it was true?
11. Franklin Delano Roosevelt served as president of the United States for four terms. After his death, a law was passed making it illegal for any president to serve

more than two terms. What do you feel was the reason for passing such a law? Do you think it is a good
law or not?

12. Franklin Delano Roosevelt was the first president to
use the radio to communicate with the American people. How do you think media like radio and television
have changed American politics? Do you think their
effect has been good, bad, or both?

13. During the New Deal, Franklin Delano Roosevelt's
administration set up codes regulating businesses.
These codes covered a variety of things including
worker safety, product control, and regulation of the
stock market. Do you feel such codes are necessary?
Why?

14. Describe three functions or responsibilities the federal
government took on for the first time during the
New Deal. How did these things change American
life? Do you think the change was positive or
negative?

Andrist, Ralph K., Editor. *The American Heritage History of the 20s and 30s.* American Heritage, 1970.

Bailey, Ronald H. and the editors of Time-Life Books. *The Home Front: USA.* Time-Life Books, 1977.

Boardman, Fon W., Jr. *America and the Jazz Age: A History of America in the 1920s.* H.Z. Walck, 1970.

Boardman, Fon W., Jr. *America and the Progressive Era: 1900–1917.* H. Z. Walck, 1968.

Burns, James MacGregor. *Roosevelt: The Soldier of Freedom, 1940–1945.* Harcourt Brace Jovanovich, 1970.

Faber, Doris. *Franklin Delano Roosevelt.* Abelard-Shuman, 1975.

Garraty, John A. *Theodore Roosevelt: The Strenuous Life.* American Heritage, 1967.

Horan, James David. *The Desperate Years: A Pictorial History of the Thirties.* Crown, 1962.

Lawson, Don. *FDR's New Deal.* Crowell, 1979.

Lindop, Edmund. *Modern America: The Turbulent Thirties.* F. Watts, 1970.

Roosevelt, Elliott and Brough, James. *The Roosevelts of Hyde Park: An Untold Story.* Putnam, 1973.

Sullivan, Wilson. *Franklin Delano Roosevelt.* American Heritage, 1970.

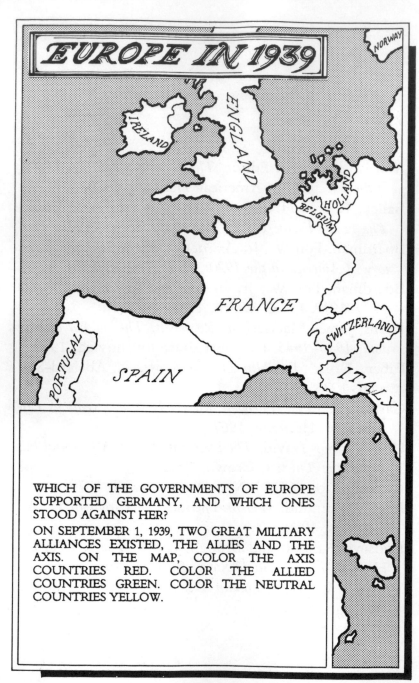

EUROPE IN 1939

NORWAY

IRELAND

ENGLAND

HOLLAND

BELGIUM

FRANCE

SWITZERLAND

PORTUGAL

SPAIN

ITALY

WHICH OF THE GOVERNMENTS OF EUROPE SUPPORTED GERMANY, AND WHICH ONES STOOD AGAINST HER?

ON SEPTEMBER 1, 1939, TWO GREAT MILITARY ALLIANCES EXISTED, THE ALLIES AND THE AXIS. ON THE MAP, COLOR THE AXIS COUNTRIES RED. COLOR THE ALLIED COUNTRIES GREEN. COLOR THE NEUTRAL COUNTRIES YELLOW.

A

Agricultural Adjustment Act,
122–123
Atlantic Charter, 138

B

Black Thursday, 108
Brain Trust, 117
Brown, Lothrop, 19, 20–21,
27

C

Campobello, 5–6, 82, 153
Churchill, Winston, 135–136,
138, 148–149, 153
Civilian Conservation Corps
(CCC), 119, 153
Civil Works Administration
(CWA), 120
Cleveland, Grover, 7–8
Coolidge, Calvin, 93
Cox, James M., 78
Crimson, 24–25, 28–29, 154

D

Daniels, Josephus, 62, 65–66,
154
D-Day, 145–146, 154
Duchess County, 48–49, 154

E

Eisenhower, Dwight D.,
144–145, 154
Emergency Banking Bill, 118

F

Farley, James, 111–112, 155
Federal Emergency Relief Act
(FERA), 119–120
Fireside Chats, 125, 143, 155
Fourteen Points Plan, 72–73,
75, 155

G

Great Depression, 108–110,
114, 118–119, 155
Groton Academy, 13–19, 155
Grotonian, 18–19, 155
Guadalcanal, 147

H

Harding, Warren G., 79, 155
Harvard Union, 29
Hitler, Adolf, 130–132, 135–
136, 145, 155
Hoover, Herbert, 109–110,
156
Hopkins, Harry, 119–120,
142, 156
Howe, Louis McHenry, 58–
60, 79, 87–88, 99, 101,
111–112, 126–127, 156